Today

Emotions Anonymous International

P.O. Box 4245
St. Paul, Minnesota
1987

— Published by —
EMOTIONS ANONYMOUS INTERNATIONAL
P.O. Box 4245
St. Paul, Minnesota 55104

First Printing   1987
Second Printing   1990
Third Printing   1991

Library of Congress Catalog Card Number: 87-081559
ISBN: 0-9607356-2-3

Today

INTRODUCTION

This book, TODAY, is intended to help us live our program one day at a time. it has been written by members of EMOTIONS ANONYMOUS for anyone who wants to spend a part of each day with a few minutes in thought, prayer, and meditation. It is our hope that these daily readings may help us find the serenity, courage, wisdom, and peace of mind so vital in our everyday lives and the world we live in TODAY.

Some Suggestions on How to Use TODAY

There is no perfect time for meditation; some prefer mornings, some evenings. It has been proved, though, that a certain amount of time set aside each day for the reading of inspirational material brings us a spiritual closeness to our Higher Power and has a relaxing and soothing effect on our physical and mental well-being.

These reflections, prayers, and inspiring thoughts can make a positive difference in your daily living if you make an effort to incorporate them into your life. This means you must *use* them. We believe the following ways of using them are the most beneficial.

1. Take a few minutes to relax before reading. Release the tensions from your day. Try closing your eyes, taking a few deep breaths, or concentrating on a peaceful thought. Whatever works for you.

2. Read the Reflection for Today. Read it slowly. Be certain you understand what you are reading.

3. Think about what you have read. Does it apply to you? Can you apply it in your daily life? How? Is this a goal you can set for yourself for today or tomorrow? How?

4. Read the Meditation (Prayer) for Today. This is a more personal contact with your Higher Power. Is there a way for you to make it even more personal?

5. Read the Today I Will Remember. Hopefully you will be able to concentrate on this last mini-thought throughout your day. It is a brief line which can help you to remember to apply the context of the whole article during the next twenty-four hours.

6. It can be helpful to have a pen and paper near as you are meditating. Writing down ways of applying personally what you have learned keeps it fresh in your mind longer.

January

January 1

REFLECTION FOR TODAY

It is the first day of a New Year. Another beginning of my new life. As I reflect upon last year. I can see many changes in me. It is not the big changes in me that are so interesting; it is the infinitesimal changes in me which count and will build the firm foundation for my future. Just as it takes many little bricks to build a firm foundation for a large building, so it is with my life. I will lay bricks one day at a time and continue to cement them with faith in my Higher Power. I shall enter into this New Year in peace knowing I am never alone and am in partnership with the Master Builder.

MEDITATION FOR TODAY

I trust You have a wonderful design for my life already drawn up.

TODAY I WILL REMEMBER

The construction of my life will go as planned just so long as I am willing to be crew and do not play architect.

January 2

The Twelve Steps make up a whole. Each is good separately but unless we apply all of them to our lives, we will regress. It is easy to enter the Program, get excited, work only a few of the Steps, and feel better for having done as much as we did. If we do not consciously make a choice to change our way of life permanently to include *all* of the Steps, we may lose what we have gained. At the least, we will not continue to progress and will lose out on the serenity promised as the result of working the Steps. It is very tempting to be satisfied with lowering the pain level to manageable proportions. If we do stop there, the person we hurt the most is ourselves although we may also hurt others. The difference between working the whole Program and only part is the difference between serenity and existing.

MEDITATION FOR TODAY

May You always remind me that, "Just for Today", I have a Program.

TODAY I WILL REMEMBER

This Program is not a menu from which to choose what I want but a way of life. To get the full benefits, I must *live* it all.

January 3

No machine can last forever without periodic maintenance. Some of this can be done while the machine is in operation - oiling, tuning, cleaning. Other types of maintenance require "down time". In working the Program, some Steps are "operating" Steps and some are more likely to be "down time" Steps. Steps 1 through 3, 10 and 12 are important in our operating maintenance. Steps 4 through 9 may require down time. Step 11 is a sort of bridge between and helps us know when down time is needed.

MEDITATION FOR TODAY

May I keep on top of what is happening enough to know when I need down time. May I plan some down time in the near future to do some preventive maintenance work on my Program.

TODAY I WILL REMEMBER

I cannot afford *not* to take periodic down time.

January 4

REFLECTION FOR TODAY

It was a relief to stop blaming myself for failing to do the impossible - to change me. It felt good to say, "I can't." Admitting I was powerless, as Step One suggests, released me from the painful chore of being responsible for the world and everyone in it. I do have a power, a Higher Power, who supports me as I make changes to better my life and become a better person, and who gives me directions for the way to remain powerless over things and other people.

MEDITATION FOR TODAY

Help me to realize Your will, for me and others, is wiser than mine.

TODAY I WILL REMEMBER

Powerlessness is not weakness; it is reality.

January 5

When I lose my balance, I instinctively reach out for something to grab on to. I am learning to pay more attention to this basic instinct and have come to see myself as a life-long toddler losing my balance in many relationships. Step Two suggests there is a power I can reach out to; one who will help me maintain my balance. It is great to know I have support. I am no longer on my own, stumbling and falling. The belief in this power gives me the stability I need in my life.

MEDITATION FOR TODAY

I am not afraid to stumble any more; Your support brings balance to my life.

TODAY I WILL REMEMBER

Believing in a Higher Power makes my life sane.

January 6

I started giving God a chance to control the outcome of things as suggested in Step Three. I
discovered when I did that, I was freer to do
what had to be done. When I remember I cannot
control the universe (not even my own little
universe), I can relax and let my Higher Power
take over the worries of my world. It is such
marvelous freedom to not be in control. The
energy I save when I turn my life over to God as
I understand God can be spent enjoying all the
good things: love, smiles, family, friends, hugs,
or nature. I have to make that conscious decision of surrender every day of my life. What a
relief!

MEDITATION FOR TODAY

I pray I continue to have the sense to turn my
life and my will over to You each morning as I
awaken.

TODAY I WILL REMEMBER

Worry is worthless; surrender is serenity.

January 7

REFLECTION FOR TODAY

I knew my secrets were hurting me a lot. As I was being hurt, I was hurting others. I finally decided to call a secret a secret and I itemized them as suggested in Step Four. I faced them with the one weapon that could get rid of them -honesty. Being honest with myself made it easier to be honest with others. Through looking at past mistakes I found I could forgive myself for being human. Isn't that what I am supposed to be? While going through this self-inventory, I found I really had some strong points. This led to a new sense of confidence. Now when I take my inventory I know I have to have done at least one good thing today - if it was only getting up on time. There were days in the past when I did not get up at all.

MEDITATION FOR TODAY

May I continue to take moral inventories of myself, never holding anything back out of shame or pride. Help me to be willing to recognize my assets.

TODAY I WILL REMEMBER

I need to accept that I have assets.

January 8

Holding onto my secrets became intolerable; sharing them was unthinkable. I shared them anyway and survived. I survived because without working suggested Step Five I could not have survived. I would have "slipped" out of the Program. I needed to get rid of all the awfulness of my past. The only way to release the sordidness, the shame, the dishonesties, and the guilt was to take a complete moral inventory of myself and to honestly admit it to God, to myself, and to another human being. I learned that burying or stuffing my attributes or failings will only do me harm. The human being I worked with was a Fifth-Step person.

MEDITATION FOR TODAY

God, help me continue to be as honest and open with others as I was at my first Fifth Step.

TODAY I WILL REMEMBER

A Fifth Step once a year is like spring cleaning; everything gets shiny and bright.

January 9

REFLECTION FOR TODAY

I came to believe that God had a sense of humor and did not hold my defects against me. We could both laugh at the fix I was in. Like a kitten tangled in yarn, if I stopped struggling, God would gradually get me untangled. I needed to stop struggling, which would help me become "entirely ready" as the Sixth Step suggests. Even as I prayed that all my defects of character be removed, I found myself thinking I was not yet able to be rid of certain ones. What would I do without this bad habit? How would I spend my time? That was the time to surrender - over and over.

MEDITATION FOR TODAY

God, please help me to deal with the character defects which brought me to my bottom. Remind me to continuously work the Steps with enthusiastic effort, which is the way to become ready.

TODAY I WILL REMEMBER

God has the power to change my life.

January 10

REFLECTION FOR TODAY

I began to exercise patience. I told myself, "My Higher Power is working on me as fast as possible." Telling God I was willing to wait made the waiting easier somehow. As Step Seven suggests, I asked for God's help through grace. When I asked for my short-comings to be removed, I found I was not giving anything up, but eliminating things which could again lead to my downfall. I was cleaning house and sending the unnecessary items to the dump - not just dusting them off and putting them back. I could not do this alone.

MEDITATION FOR TODAY

May I take action and not just pray and wait by using the EA tools which have so graciously been given to me.

TODAY I WILL REMEMBER

I will clean my mental house from the inside out and ask God to be my "trashman".

January 11

REFLECTION FOR TODAY

I became aware that in my struggles I had elbowed a lot of people in the ribs. Many of them I had hammered in the heart as well. I realized that in order to live in peace with everyone, I had to make an honest and accurate list of all those I had harmed as suggested in Step Eight. It was hard to face the fact that my behavior had affected so many others. It was easier when a friend suggested my own name be at the top of my list. As I gathered the names together, I asked God to help me become willing to make amends to all, including me.

MEDITATION FOR TODAY

May You continue to give me the honesty, courage, and humility necessary for me to take the responsibility for my actions so I am always willing to make amends.

TODAY I WILL REMEMBER

I cannot do good or bad to others without doing good or bad to myself.

January 12

I became more mannerly and stopped thinking it was all right to hurt people around me. It became easier to say things such as, "Excuse me. I didn't mean to bump into you." I became aware that there were others around me as sensitive as I was. As Step Nine suggests, I began to make direct amends to the people I had harmed whenever it was possible. Fear and pride made it difficult at first and I had to be willing to risk. It became easier as my apologies were accepted. Some people had died and others had moved away so I asked God to help with those amends. Making amends releases guilt feelings.

MEDITATION FOR TODAY

God, please grant me the courage, honesty, and good sense to enable me to sincerely and lovingly apologize, including to myself.

TODAY I WILL REMEMBER

Everybody can be hurt including me.

January 13

By now I can safely assume I am going to make mistakes as long as I live. They are a nuisance, but they have become an increasingly familiar nuisance. I think I would miss them now if they suddenly vanished. When I admit my mistakes, it is like welcoming my inlaws - they are a pain in the rear, but they are a part of me and I have learned to love them (a little). As Step Ten suggests, if I continue to take personal inventory, I can catch the mistakes almost as soon as I make them and then promptly admit them - to myself and others.

MEDITATION FOR TODAY

May I remember to regularly work Step Ten to guard against old behavior patterns creeping into my life. Help me to take responsibility for my mistakes and to face the consequences which are the result.

TODAY I WILL REMEMBER

The biggest mistake I can make is to not search out my mistakes.

January 14

God has become a bigger and bigger part of my life - not because I am so devoted, but because I am seeing God in more and more places. I began by talking to and asking God questions, sort of getting acquainted. I don't need to worry about proper words and flowery phrases. This new friend of mine understands what I am saying and even what I am not saying. I believe God lovingly watches over me. I believe this Higher Power of mine is my friend, my partner, and my constant companion. These beliefs come to me because of working Step Eleven.

MEDITATION FOR TODAY

May I keep seeking, as suggested in Step Eleven, to improve my conscious contact with You.

TODAY I WILL REMEMBER

Not my will, but Thine.

January 15

Step Twelve is a hard Step for me to do deliberately. I think I do it best when I allow myself to be just myself. It is much easier for me now to share myself with others. I have to be able to Twelfth-Step myself before I can carry the message. By practicing the principles of the Program in all my affairs, I become a living example of a better life. When I share my experiences, strengths, and hope with newcomers, I, in turn, give them hope. Hope gives us all a reason to live and with that comes strength to go on.

MEDITATION FOR TODAY

May I always be the best possible example to others. May my past experiences and future goals give them and me the willingness to work harder to achieve and maintain emotional health.

TODAY I WILL REMEMBER

I cannot keep it unless I give it away.

January 16

God gave us the changing seasons to remind us that all of life will be filled with constant change. I will never be the same person that I was yesterday and tomorrow I will change some more from what I am today. The snows of winter give way to flowers in the spring. So it will be with my life. If I stay close to God, the drab winters of my life will eventually give way to beautiful flowers. Neither the flowers nor the trees fear the coming of winter. They follow the dictates of God and trust that their changes will evolve into new beauty and life.

MEDITATION FOR TODAY

I pray that I may take lessons from nature and not worry about the wintry days nor fear any changes in my life.

TODAY I WILL REMEMBER

Spring ALWAYS follows winter.

January 17

Has my life become more manageable since I came into this Program? Even if it has not, I have an ingredient which I did not have before: HOPE. Hope alone is something I never used to have. Even though I am still powerless on my own, I have learned there is a power I can reach out to. If other people in the group have been able to find new life, then I can hope to find it too. I am now able to look forward to better things ahead.

MEDITATION FOR TODAY

May I count every small victory as a big step in my life.

TODAY I WILL REMEMBER

I have hope for today.

January 18

"My problem is not powerlessness, but too much power over my emotions," I said. Then I learned that controlled emotions control me. "Of all emotions, I relate to anger least," I said. Then I learned that my large choices in life, no less than my idlest snap judgements of people, were ruled by unadmitted angers and fears. "How inappropriate their angers are," I said of my near ones. But my own poor strategies of living had gone to produce the emotional climate I complain against. I learned detachment and forgiveness.

MEDITATION FOR TODAY

May my love for others continue to grow as I learn to acknowledge my true feelings and to accept the consequences of my feelings in the real world.

TODAY I WILL REMEMBER

I will listen to my feelings and direct them toward recovery.

January 19

REFLECTION FOR TODAY

There are some days when I do not feel capable of meeting any challenges. There are some days when I do not feel confident and wish I had more abilities. Those are the days when I have to remind myself often that I *can* meet challenges and *can* accomplish whatever I have to do; that I *do* have the ability to make good decisions. I need to remind myself that my Higher Power and I are greater than any challenge. When we are working together, I am capable of using my God-given talents and abilities, and nothing can interfere with my success.

MEDITATION FOR TODAY

Help me to remember that You and I can handle anything.

TODAY I WILL REMEMBER

To begin each day with a positive attitude because I know I can rely on my Partner.

January 20

REFLECTION FOR TODAY

By being kind, considerate, and generous as a pleaser, I was looking for acceptance. I put the responsibility on the other person to make me feel good about myself instead of on my own shoulders where it belonged. I am not saying I should never do anything for another, but I need to continually be aware of my motives. Does what I am doing violate my values? Do I have strings attached? Am I expecting something back? Am I doing it only because I want someone to like me?

MEDITATION FOR TODAY

Let me be more aware of my motives for doing what I choose to do. I no longer want to lose myself for I am all I really have.

TODAY I WILL REMEMBER

If I continue to exist for others, I will not gain; instead, I will lose the most precious gift God has given me - myself.

January 21

I once overheard it said the way you can tell a spiritual thing from something material is in sharing. When you share something material, the more you share it the smaller portion each person gets. On the other hand, when you share something spiritual, its value is simply multiplied by the number of persons with whom you share. They may in turn share it thus increasing it a thousandfold. The principles of this Program are spiritual and to persevere in "giving it away to keep it" sooner or later makes the promises come true of having a new and better way of life.

MEDITATION FOR TODAY

May I focus on one of the Steps today and share it with someone.

TODAY I WILL REMEMBER

I can't give it if I don't have it.

January 22

Storm clouds are often ominously black on the bottom. They suggest rain, lightening, thunder, and what is generally considered "bad" weather. They also suggest eventual rainbows, fresh air, and healthy crops. Our problems are much the same. They are ominous to face. But, if we can detach ourselves from them, they do not engender fear. Just as we can enjoy a thunderstorm by anticipating the peace and sense of well being which is to follow, we can approach the problems we face with hope in our hearts. Sometimes we may need to take shelter during our storms. It makes no more sense to seek trouble than it does to go into a raging storm when it is not necessary.

MEDITATION FOR TODAY

Be my rain gear to get me through the storms I face.

TODAY I WILL REMEMBER

"This too shall pass" can be my weather report. I may not see the rainbow until after the storm.

January 23

REFLECTION FOR TODAY

Today I will take care of myself. For me that was a totally new concept. I have discovered I am important enough that I do not have to please anybody but me. If I try to please everybody, there is no guarantee anybody will be pleased. If I please myself, at least one person will be happy.

MEDITATION FOR TODAY

May I reflect on the value of the EA Program which taught me my worth as a person. May I thank You daily for me.

TODAY I WILL REMEMBER

I do not need to be a people pleaser, but I shall try to remember it is a pleasure to be around people who are pleasant.

January 24

REFLECTION FOR TODAY

Sex is a topic which is not often talked about with sincerity and honesty. Those of us who have come to EA often find as part of our recovery a need to deal with some unhealthy attitudes about sex. Many peoples' attitudes about sex seem to go from one extreme to the other; either it is dirty or it is an obsession. Sharing our sexual struggles with the group will lead to healthier outlooks.

MEDITATION FOR TODAY

God, when I am afraid to share with the group, may I have the courage to confide in a trustworthy member or a Fifth Step person. That can be a beginning.

TODAY I WILL REMEMBER

As I continue to face myself, I continue to become more whole.

January 25

Before EA I took on the responsibility of feeling loved ones' pain when they were hurting. For days I would obsessively try to think of the magic sentence or idea which would solve their problems immediately. Now I realize I do not have that power and knowledge, so I immediately turn another's tough situation over to God. My attitude now is: if God wants me to be helpful in a situation, it will flow naturally with no obsessiveness or self-will on my part. Most times it is love and compassion which God wills me to give to the one in pain; not a direct solution to their problem(s).

MEDITATION FOR TODAY

Please help me to let go of any situation I have been tightly hanging on to.

TODAY I WILL REMEMBER

Emotional releasing of a problem is the first step towards a situation in which I feel powerless.

January 26

Too often we have been hesitant to express ourselves. Fearing rejection, our own or another's, we withdrew. The more we closed off, the more lonely and fearful we became. Before we were willing to risk sharing ourselves, many of us needed to hear over and over again that expressing our feelings is a sign of being healthy. When we are finally able to tell someone what we are feeling, we experience relief and often jubilation. Someone's acceptance gives us the courage to risk once again.

MEDITATION FOR TODAY

May I be willing to risk sharing who I am with someone today.

TODAY I WILL REMEMBER

Only through self-disclosure do we discover the beauty of self.

January 27

REFLECTION FOR TODAY

An example of a morning meditation is: "My God, I surrender my life, my will, and my love to you this day. I offer the day up to You and hope it is worthy of Your love. Please direct and protect my family and their families as well as all friends. Direct and protect those whom I resent and help me to forgive them. Help all in need of solace and friendship. May my family and I stay in good health and may I do my best at work with efficiency, intelligence, patience, tolerance, and energy. I am so grateful to You for my many blessings."

MEDITATION FOR TODAY

If I forget to start my day with a mediation, please remind me how important it is for me.

TODAY I WILL REMEMBER

Every day is better when I start it by communicating with my Higher Power.

January 28

It is possible to get rid of that "poor little ol' me" feeling if I make up my mind to do so. When that "feel sorry for myself for no reason" syndrome comes my way, I do have the ability to change my attitude. First I take a few moments to concentrate on what is bothering me. If I can not come up with a legitimate reason for the "blues", it is time to take action. I tell myself I have ten minutes to really wallow in self-pity and set the clock to ring at that time. I play sad records and dwell on the injustices of life. When the alarm goes off, I ask my Higher Power for help to concentrate on positive thoughts which lead to my feeling better about myself. The key here is I can change my moods with my Higher Power's help and some concentrated effort on my part.

MEDITATION FOR TODAY

Thank You for the ability to switch from negative to positive thinking.

TODAY I WILL REMEMBER

I can mope when I want to, but only for ten minutes.

January 29

REFLECTION FOR TODAY

Sometimes I feel real joy, like today. It is sunny and very cold, the kind of day I enjoy very much, and I would much rather be outside in it instead of inside looking out my window. Somehow, the brightness of the day says to me that part of emotional healing lies in knowledge and awareness. If I am to solve the problems I have, I feel I can best do it in the bright light of accurate knowledge. Since I do want to solve my problems, awareness will help.

MEDITATION FOR TODAY

Help me to seek the bright light of awareness and the knowledge of what and where I am.

TODAY I WILL REMEMBER

Only through self-acceptance can I bear to take a true look inside myself.

January 30

REFLECTION FOR TODAY

When I see greeting cards that say, "Happy birthday from your secret pal" or "Best wishes from your secret pal," I have to chuckle to myself. I have a secret pal - one who does not send cards on special occasions but one who makes every day special if I only remember to ask and to surrender my problems. My secret pal is my Higher Power and everyone else can have the same friend I do. The key for me is to start each day by turning my life over and asking for serenity and acceptance for the day. If, in my haste to get going in the morning I do not take the time for my surrender, it is not long before I realize the day is not going well. It is then time for action.

MEDITATION FOR TODAY

May I not forget it is never too late in the day to turn my life over to You.

TODAY I WILL REMEMBER

Greeting cards are always special but successful days are my Secret Pal's specialty.

January 31

REFLECTION FOR TODAY

Self-acceptance is one of the important parts of the EA Program for me. I am learning to love and accept myself through the Twelve Steps. I am learning I do not have to be perfect....only human. I have assets as well as defects, as everyone does. I am reminded of the story of the three-legged stool. One leg is our love and acceptance of ourselves. The second leg is God's love and acceptance. And the third leg is our love and acceptance of other people. What a wonderful life I have when I can experience all three of the "legs". I am learning about acceptance. When I feel God's love and acceptance, I am able to love and accept myself. What follows is a love and acceptance of others.

MEDITATION FOR TODAY

God, help me to feel Your love and acceptance. May I be the kind of person You want to be. May I learn what Your will is for me and accept it.

TODAY I WILL REMEMBER

My daily spiritual reading and interchange with others is important in helping me feel the presence of God.

February

February 1

REFLECTION FOR TODAY

We are afraid of failure and also afraid of success. With success comes a responsibility to self and to others. We can best handle success by turning to our Higher Power with gratitude. We may also be afraid of falling on our face again. What will people think? We may feel we need to live up to some image, but we do not. Even if we do stumble and fall, and ultimately we will, we will be given the strength to once again pick ourselves up. We will gain more humility, we will learn from our falling, and we will become stronger and more capable.

MEDITATION FOR TODAY

May I realize You are with me to help me handle success, too.

TODAY I WILL REMEMBER

An attitude of gratitude will keep our success in perspective.

February 2

In the northern part of the United States we honor a kind of silly tradition called Groundhog Day on this date. As the legend goes, this small animal comes out of hibernation to see if he can see his shadow. If the sun is shining, he runs back into his hole and that is supposed to mean six more weeks of winter, which no one wants. The groundhog reminds me of myself in my pre-program days - afraid of my own shadow. I was afraid of my past, my present, and my future. I believed the remainder of my life would be all winter. There was no love to warm me or any hope to kindle a spark of energy to set my inner furnace working. I have learned I have nothing to be afraid of because I have a Higher Power to turn to. My life has grown to include all four seasons: summer, fall, winter, and spring.

MEDITATION FOR TODAY

Help me realize the seasons come from my heart and mind.

TODAY I WILL REMEMBER

Life is fuller with all four seasons.

February 3

REFLECTION FOR TODAY

Intimacy is not referring only to sexual relationships. Intimacy is being very close to someone: someone we trust, someone with whom we can share our deepest thoughts and feelings. We all need an intimate relationship, even those who might vehemently express they do not. To have someone truly know us and still accept us gives us the human bonding we need to find our existence meaningful. We are loveable. We do count. We are worthwhile. Yet we will never come to this realization unless we leave the door to our heart open.

MEDITATION FOR TODAY

May I have the humility to be myself and let someone close know something I have been hiding.

TODAY I WILL REMEMBER

Each time we risk being vulnerable and are accepted, we feel loved. We also discover a greater awareness of our value.

February 4

Many of us at one time or another have been perfectionists. This has led to excessive activity, oppression of others, or even to paralysis of action. The Slogan "Let Go and Let God" does not mean to quit. It means to leave the results to God. If we can do that and concern ourselves only with the effort, we will accomplish a great deal. At the same time we can be happy since we will avoid anxiety.

MEDITATION FOR TODAY
I pray I will only consider doing my best - that is perfect enough for me.

TODAY I WILL REMEMBER
Perfect is not necessarily best.

February 5

REFLECTION FOR TODAY

I am full of contradictions. I am angry and I am loving. I am happy about some things and I am often sad about the same things. I love and hate some people. I seek and fear success. This, to a logical person, is almost impossible to deal with. To ancient man it was confusing that there were seasons. Lightening was a mystery prior to Ben Franklin. Neither of these ideas baffles us today. I am now learning to accept the contradictions within me as things I just do not understand.

MEDITATION FOR TODAY

Help me to realize that understanding comes with time.

TODAY I WILL REMEMBER

I will be shown.

February 6

REFLECTION FOR TODAY

I decide on a daily basis to surrender my will and my life (my thoughts and my actions) to God. This Step is one of total surrender. I am saying, "My life is Yours, God. I am willing to do Your will for me." My job is to pay attention for God does let me know what is wanted from me as I go through my day. Much of the time it is taking care of ordinary activities. I call it putting one foot in front of the other.

MEDITATION FOR TODAY

May I have the willingness to surrender all aspects of my life to my loving Higher Power.

TODAY I WILL REMEMBER

Surrender!

February 7

REFLECTION FOR TODAY

Today I am happy. I am happy because I am me. I am happy because my life is filled with wonders: people; places; and things. I am happy because I know I have much to give and much to receive. Today is an extraordinary day. I am happy because wonderful things are going to happen to me today. I will have new, satisfying, productive ideas and experiences. I will meet loving people who will share themselves with me. Someone will give me a hug or a warm touch and a smile. There will be laughter, sunshine, and serenity - even if it rains.

MEDITATION FOR TODAY

I give thanks for this day and bless every moment of it.

TODAY I WILL REMEMBER

I am happy!

February 8

I am a "caretaker". I thought I knew what was best for everyone. They would be fine if they would only follow my advice. When they did not, I became frustrated and angry and felt rejected. The Program teaches me that God is in charge, not me. I resent other people trying to control me, why shouldn't other people resent my trying to control them? I am not God. I am powerless to change anyone but myself. When I get too busy in other peoples' lives, it is because I am running away from myself.

MEDITATION FOR TODAY

May I remember that if I quit running the world, control will revert to the Power who is and should be in control - You.

TODAY I WILL REMEMBER

I am not in charge. God is.

February 9

I have some secret goals, some things I long to do, and yet fear often holds me back. It can be fear of failure or fear of success. I keep saying, "I can't" to myself. Saying or thinking, "I can't" certainly limits me. That is the time to start saying, "I want to, and with my Higher Power's help, I can!" Nothing is impossible with the help of my Higher Power. I can get all the strength I need, all the ability I need, and all the confidence I need. I can be free, happy, healthy, loving, and successful. I can be all I was created to be.

MEDITATION FOR TODAY

Thanks for all the help You give me when I ask and when I do not. Remind me never to take that help for granted.

TODAY I WILL REMEMBER

I want to and I can!

February 10

REFLECTION FOR TODAY

When speaking with friends in the Program, we must always remember to protect the information they share with us. By the same token, we need not hesitate to remind them of our need for privacy. It is so easy for us to speak of intimate details with EA friends that anyone can sometimes forget he or she is expected to remain silent. There are many advantages to having these free and easy conversations: we learn to be honest, we do not have to worry about ridicule or condemnation, and we have the opportunity to spot self-deception.

MEDITATION FOR TODAY

Help me to be a trusted confident - one with whom others will want to share.

TODAY I WILL REMEMBER

It is better to be a receiver than a transmitter.

February 11

One of the best persons to help you in times of trouble is someone who has had a similar problem. We say similar because no two problems are exactly alike. But somebody who has been down the path, around the track, and has actually survived to see the light at the end of the tunnel can do wonders to lighten the load of the burden we are carrying. My words, my attitudes, my caring, and my sharing are all appreciated by someone. Some times they let me know I have helped them and some times they do not. The important thing is that we help each other.

MEDITATION FOR TODAY

Open my eyes to see friends who can help me and friends I can help.

TODAY I WILL REMEMBER

A helping hand does not end at your wrist; it goes all the way to your heart.

February 12

What am I struggling with today? Do I still have some characteristics I wish to be rid of? I must be patient. God will give me all the strength I need to deal with my problems one day at a time. The solutions may not come immediately. If I get too anxious and try to take back control, I will only meet with frustration and self-hate due to what I feel is my personal failure. One small step forward, firmly planted, will be better than making two giant strides, only to trip and fall backward three steps.

MEDITATION FOR TODAY

I pray that You will show me which roads to go down first and that each step I take will be firmly planted with trust.

TODAY I WILL REMEMBER

If all else fails, try a little patience!

February 13

REFLECTION FOR TODAY

When I came to the Program, Step Three was confusing to me. Now I have learned that even though I may not totally understand God, or the meaning of God's will, I can still make a decision to surrender. I have already proved to myself that I alone cannot manage my life. What image I have of a Higher Power is not important. It is best that I just make a decision on whether I want God in my life or not. What have I got to lose?

MEDITATION FOR TODAY

If I cannot manage to say anything else, then just let me be able to say, "Help me."

TODAY I WILL REMEMBER

Stop analyzing - start accepting!

February 14

Today is a special day celebrated by lovers in the United States. The heart is a symbol which has been seen in stores for weeks. Sweethearts send each other cards, flowers, candy. We call friends and relatives to say, "Hi, I am thinking of you." We care for each other in a special way on this day. We make an effort to be nice to friends and strangers alike. In short, the day is dedicated to love. Why only one day of the year? I can strive for two days and then three and so on. In the past I was afraid to show love for fear of rejection. It is not as hard as it used to be. I have seen how necessary love is to me.

MEDITATION FOR TODAY

Help me to not be fearful of sharing my love and friendship all year long.

TODAY I WILL REMEMBER

Lack of love will pain me much more than lots of love.

February 15

REFLECTION FOR TODAY

No matter what my problem is today, no matter my mood, and no matter the weather, I can find something to be happy about if I put my mind to it. I can search for and find something to be thankful for if it is only that I got out of bed this morning. It is not God who NEEDS to be thanked, but I who need to be grateful. This gratitude fills my heart and gives me a new spirit. I give myself a fantastic reward - a thankful heart which fills a great need.

MEDITATION FOR TODAY

Fill me with a spirit of thankfulness.

TODAY I WILL REMEMBER

Thank and be thankful.

February 16

REFLECTION FOR TODAY

"...we aim for an atmosphere of love and acceptance." This helpful Concept tells me how to behave toward the newcomer to my chapter who is almost certainly hurting and who may be behaving in a way I do not like. But isn't this Concept important in my other relationships too? If I threaten to reject people in an attempt to get them to change their behavior, I am not loving, I am manipulating. Only by giving my love freely can I create the atmosphere in which I wish to live.

MEDITATION FOR TODAY

Help me to love others and to wish them their highest good even when this conflicts with my own plans or wishes.

TODAY I WILL REMEMBER

The love I give without strings attached mysteriously returns to me.

February 17

REFLECTION FOR TODAY

We are not here to judge each other, but to accept each other. God is our only judge and so much kinder to us than we are to ourselves. Many times in the past we judged others. But were we equipped to make these judgements? Do we know what brought another to take a certain action? We judge others because we are so harsh with ourselves. The more we can accept our own failures and weaknesses, the more likely we will cease to judge others.

MEDITATION FOR TODAY

May I realize that if I am judging another, it is only a sign of my own self-rejection.

TODAY I WILL REMEMBER

As I begin to talk kindly to myself, I will experience an inner peace and calmness. It will show in how I treat others.

February 18

REFLECTION FOR TODAY

As I attempt to live the Twelve Step Program, I find my focus redirected from the crippling effects of negative feelings and begin to see myself as part of a larger world. No longer must I exaggerate my self-importance or diminish my self-worth in my relationships with others. I am growing in my ability to recognize reality and I am beginning to feel good about my part in the real world.

MEDITATION FOR TODAY

Remind me that my Program offers me a blueprint for positive action.

TODAY I WILL REMEMBER

Life can be a prison if I lock myself away from others and dwell on my own negativity.

February 19

REFLECTION FOR TODAY

How painful it is at times to make choices. We want the best of both worlds. Yet most of the time this simply cannot be. We need to give up one thing to gain something else. As we seek guidance from our Higher Power and from our friends, we are helped to see the choice which will bring us our greatest good. The feeling of loss is also real and we need to acknowledge this pain. By facing our pain we are able to let go of the loss and go on once again.

MEDITATION FOR TODAY

May I have the courage to get off the fence and make a choice.

TODAY I WILL REMEMBER

As I focus on the growth my loss created, the pain of the loss will dissipate.

February 20

REFLECTION FOR TODAY

How often have we been grateful for our fear, pain, or anger? Most of us would have to say rarely. Through the Program we have come to realize these experiences are necessary to our growth and freedom, and we became more accepting of these moments. The more quickly we embrace our fear, pain, or anger, the less time we spend suffering. Our willingness to risk facing our feelings, as frightening as it often is, brings us the feelings of peace and belonging which we have been seeking for so long.

MEDITATION FOR TODAY

Grant me the courage to face my pain and the insight to see the healing beyond.

TODAY I WILL REMEMBER

I will choose to embrace my pain. I will become me.

February 21

Obstacles that are sent my way may not have a lesson in them which I can learn the same day. The patience I learn will help me to realize the master plan of life very often includes lessons for tomorrow, not today. If something is missing in my life, my Higher Power is working for my good now, and the good that will come takes time, even years in some cases, for me to get ready for it.

MEDITATION FOR TODAY

May I realize when a bad day has passed, things never look as black afterwards, especially if I deal with it by a healthy sharing with people I trust.

TODAY I WILL REMEMBER

This too shall pass means that things will get better or I will get better. It does not always mean the situation will change.

February 22

Maybe my fear comes from thinking that someone is "out to get me" because of what she/he said or did. The only way I am going to calm that fear is by talking to the person and telling her/him how I feel. I have been amazed to find that usually the other person is surprised I interpreted the words or actions the way I did because that had not been what was meant. My fear was groundless, but I never would have known if I had not asked.

MEDITATION FOR TODAY

May I remember that most of my fears come from my own negative thinking. I ask for the courage to seek clarification.

TODAY I WILL REMEMBER

Ask.

February 23

REFLECTION FOR TODAY

How many times have we all made statements like the following? "I'll save the good crystal and china for when special company comes." "When I get a bigger house my life will be better." "When I get enough money and can retire, I will be happy." We are projecting happiness into the future and forgetting that today is the day to be happy. Today is our day that God has given us to live and enjoy. The present moment is an opportunity for us to make use of our assets and enter into life with vim, vigor, and vitality.

MEDITATION FOR TODAY

May I always remember to live in and enjoy each of life's precious moments.

TODAY I WILL REMEMBER

Live for the now!

February 24

REFLECTION FOR TODAY

Am I identifying life as depression, anxiety, or another symptom? Am I afraid that if this unpleasantness were taken from me there would be nothing left? Am I truly willing to have my misery taken away? Have I embraced a *new* way of life? Have I stopped picturing myself as an emotional cripple with the implication that I can never hope to recover? Do I acknowledge God? Or do I worship and hold onto my self-pity and fear to change?

MEDITATION FOR TODAY

May my eyes be opened to the difference between accepting myself as I am today, able to change, or believing that I cannot and should not ever change. Help me to know I am, and have a choice to be, more than my pain.

TODAY I WILL REMEMBER

I will have the courage to accept the peace of the Program.

February 25

REFLECTION FOR TODAY

If I have been working my Program so long I think my bad times are over and I can control my life and my emotions, then I am probably close to a slip. None of us is immune to slipping. If I think I no longer need help, I may already be in trouble. I will always be powerless over my emotions. But as long as I take good care of myself and deal with my negative attitudes, I can have serenity.

MEDITATION FOR TODAY

May I take joy and pride in my emotional stability, but may my Higher Power also protect me from smugness.

TODAY I WILL REMEMBER

I am powerless over my emotions.

February 26

REFLECTION FOR TODAY

"You are not alone". This slogan is so important yet I often defeat it by my attitude. I cultivate loneliness by refusing to make a telephone call, by avoiding conversation at the EA meeting, or by failing to tell even my best friend how I feel. I say I have no friends. The truth is I have many friends but I treat them as strangers. When I am angry, I do not want other people in my life, and yet I blame them for not being there.

MEDITATION FOR TODAY

May I have the humility to risk inviting others to come a little closer into my life.

TODAY I WILL REMEMBER

I will not nourish my own loneliness by withdrawing from others.

February 27

REFLECTION FOR TODAY

When I am lost in Me-ness, thinking only of myself, what I am really doing is demanding the powers and privileges of a Higher Power. I expect all my plans to turn out just as I want them to. I demand that all my desires be satisfied, that I am perfect in all I do, that others do what I want them to do. In short, I demand that *My* will be done. Never am I more irrational, more grandiose, and more out of touch with my humanness.

MEDITATION FOR TODAY

May I learn to embrace my own humanness instead of futilely trying to transcend it. May I become an accepting person rather than a frustrated, would-be God. May Thy will be done instead of *Mine*.

TODAY I WILL REMEMBER

I deserve to be human - no more, no less.

February 28

REFLECTION FOR TODAY

It seems so easy to pull up stakes, move to a different house, job, or town and believe miracles will happen and that our lives will change for the better simply because of the move. We tend to forget that wherever we go, we take US. We take our emotions, our feelings, and everything we are made of. The only thing which will make our lives better is to change us - inside. We are the only ones who can do this - with God's help. We must do away with the negative attitudes and change to positive thinking. No external *thing* can make us happy.

MEDITATION FOR TODAY

Help me to change my attitudes so serenity gets easier to find.

TODAY I WILL REMEMBER

Geographic changes alone will not enhance my life.

February 29

REFLECTION FOR TODAY

Today is a very unique day; it only comes to me once every four years. It is, in a sense, an extra day - a special treat. What can I do to make this day really count? How shall I take advantage of the twenty-four hours? I can begin by making a commitment to be more accepting of others. I shall be more loving - of myself, as well as those around me. And I will take the time to enjoy my surroundings and the events which occur throughout this time. I will close this novel period of my life with gratitude to my Higher Power for one more wonderful day of living.

MEDITATION FOR TODAY

Thank You for an extra special day.

TODAY I WILL REMEMBER

God gave me a perfect gift of twenty-four hours and asked for nothing in return.

March

March 1

REFLECTION FOR TODAY

Our incessant analyzing could mean our failure to get well and eventually cost us our lives. It is as if we were standing in a burning fire trying to understand the principles of oxidation, and how or why the fire might have started before we make plans for escape. What we need to do is get out of the fire first and try to understand later. For a long time we will stand on the edge of our old lives and think about going back. Have I made a clear choice?

MEDITATION FOR TODAY

May I learn how to relate to You rather than to my analytical mind.

TODAY I WILL REMEMBER

Stop analyzing. Act!

March 2

Today, God, I may need a little extra special help. I know I have asked You to step in and take care of this problem which is bothering me. Please help me to understand that You may solve it differently from the way I expected. That way I will know even if adversities come while You are working Your solution, they will not throw me into thinking that You have deserted me.

MEDITATION FOR TODAY

I have turned my life over to Your care, God, and I need extra attention today.

TODAY I WILL REMEMBER

I am worthy of special help.

March 3

REFLECTION FOR TODAY

As I think about the day that lies ahead of me, what do I visualize? Do I think only about negative things such as gloomy weather, hard work, and confrontations? If I expect good, good will come my way. I must start out the day expecting it to be a happy day. I know I will rejoice in good happenings. I expect tranquility, serenity, and friendliness. I will feel love and give love to others this day. Delightful surprises will come my way. I will be blessed with vigor and good health. In moments of quiet and prayer, I will feel peace and know my Higher Power is with me.

MEDITATION FOR TODAY

Thank You for the gift of another joyful day.

TODAY I WILL REMEMBER

Great expectations bring a great day.

March 4

We may talk about love, define love, read books about love, and see movies about love but still not *be* loving. One way to start being loving is to love what bothers you. Is there a person who irritates and angers you? Think: I love you and God bless you. Is there someone you resent? Think: I love you and God bless you. Do you fear a person who seems to stand in the way of your good? Let love eliminate the fear. Think: I love you and God bless you. You may at first be thinking I love you with tight lips and clenched fists. As it gets to be habit, love takes over and the words truly become meaningful.

MEDITATION FOR TODAY

May I become more loving and only see Your gift of love in the people I meet today.

TODAY I WILL REMEMBER

Love erases fear, anger, and resentments.

March 5

REFLECTION FOR TODAY

For many years of my life I thought I was lacking in talent. Because I had focused on others' abilities, I could not see my own. Of course this created a feeling of jealousy. I realize now I no longer have to be jealous of someone else's ability. God's talent to one person does not limit another's abilities. We each are given more than enough to make our lives full and rewarding. If we are willing to take the risk and follow where we are being led, we will discover abilities we did not know we possessed.

MEDITATION FOR TODAY

May I have the courage to follow my dream with action.

TODAY I WILL REMEMBER

Courage is a choice!

March 6

REFLECTION FOR TODAY

Nothing is scarier than the unknown so naturally letting go of symptoms and old behavior was frightening. Even though I was miserable, I wondered what would replace this void. Recognizing that the energy I had put into keeping my symptoms alive was energy I could also use to develop my creativity gave me a great deal of hope for the positive direction my life could take. When the fear of returning to the pain of my self-defeating behavior became greater than my fear of the unknown, it was easier to face that fear. Little by little I let go of my old ways.

MEDITATION FOR TODAY

May I continue to use my energy to grow, to be responsible, and to be creative. May I no longer let fear control my life.

TODAY I WILL REMEMBER

By giving up self-defeating behavior, I will not become just an empty vessel.

March 7

REFLECTION FOR TODAY

Anger can get me into trouble and pride can keep me there. Admitting I am wrong is hard as I want to be perfect, keep my world all intact, and not lose control. I am not alone in the world any more. I am a human being living a life which is the best I know and I do not have to be perfect. I can make mistakes and then correct the error without being a failure.

MEDITATION FOR TODAY

May I have more patience and tolerance which will lead to improved relations with You and others.

TODAY I WILL REMEMBER

Honesty is a powerful tool to eliminate false pride.

March 8

If there is no joy or enthusiasm in my life, it can seem to be a pretty bleak and depressing world I live in. Where there is no color in my life, there is no rainbow either. By bringing enthusiasm into my everyday work, I add color and spice. Today I will be enthusiastic in doing whatever I have to do. I will speak and act enthusiastically. This can uplift me all day. And it rubs off on others! When I am joyful, people around me feel better. Only I can do this for me. The good feelings it gives to others are a bonus which I receive for being good to myself. And the amount of work accomplished is incredible - another bonus.

MEDITATION FOR TODAY

Help me to put rainbows into my life by granting me the strength for enthusiasm.

TODAY I WILL REMEMBER

The pot of gold at the end of my rainbow is joy.

March 9

REFLECTION FOR TODAY

Could I go a whole day, a whole twenty-four hours without "trying to improve or regulate anybody except myself?" It does not seem like a difficult task. After all, *I am* the only one *I can* change. Yet why do I expend so much of my energy on trying to change others? How do I know what is good for another person? Most of the time I don't know what is good for me. Today I will try extremely hard to accept other people regardless of their behavior. Today I will concentrate on my qualities, bad or good, and let the other person be an individual with human foibles. If this dedication to myself only works five hours today, maybe it will last six hours tomorrow and I will have taken another giant step on my path toward serenity.

MEDITATION FOR TODAY

Help me to let You make all the improvements on the human race.

TODAY I WILL REMEMBER

During this day I will accept others as they are; human, just like me, and entitled to their humanity.

March 10

REFLECTION FOR TODAY

I used to view success as outward achievements and material gains. Today success looks much different. Real success is not external, but internal. Each time I risk and challenge something, I learn more about myself, and I feel successful. By facing myself, I gain more and more understanding and acceptance of both my strengths and my weaknesses. This understanding creates compassion. To gain compassion for one's self is to achieve success. Only by being compassionate with ourselves will we keep the door open to continued growth.

MEDITATION FOR TODAY

Because I understand how imperative having compassion for myself is to my continued growth, I pray for the ability to talk kindly to myself instead of being self-rejecting.

TODAY I WILL REMEMBER

If we have not learned to live with ourselves, what benefit are achievements and material gains?

March 11

After one year of working my own Program I came to realize that one thing I was not hearing or seeing but definitely needed to cultivate within myself was *acceptance*. It is one thing to accept the first three Steps which address the problem. It is another to take that Fourth and Fifth Step and accept those things intrinsic to one's personality. Accepting major personality factors does not mean to qualify them as good, bad, or defective. However, the admission I make in Step Five opens the dike I have built between myself and reality. It starts like the small hole in the fable which day by day grows larger giving me an increasing awareness of the goodness within myself which I have refused to accept. Am I working a Three Step or a Twelve Step Program?

MEDITATION FOR TODAY

Please, God, do not allow me to bog down in my Program. Let it be Your will that I continue in the Steps and grow strong and able to accept myself and what is to come.

TODAY I WILL REMEMBER

God does not make anything that ain't good.

March 12

REFLECTION FOR TODAY

I have done myself a lot of harm but I want to make amends to myself now. One of the best ways to do this is to continually speak well of myself. Why do I think I am entitled to run myself down, saying harsh things about myself such as, "I am no good, I cannot do it, I am so weak, nobody cares about me, etc."? Without dishonesty or conceit I can always speak positively and hopefully about myself. Today I want to be my own best friend.

MEDITATION FOR TODAY

May I remember there are people who love and cherish me and it hurts them as it hurts me when I say negative things about myself.

TODAY I WILL REMEMBER

I am not perfect but in some ways I am great.

March 13

The God of my understanding - how it has changed through the years. When I was a child He was a man with a beard who patted me on the head when I was good. In my teens He disapproved of most things I thought were fun so He probably did not exist. In my twenties I had children so I thought I better teach them about God in case He did exist. Now I am past forty, God is not a man. My Creator is a force for good, a loving friend, a support when I call, the one who accepts me when I cannot, and the one who always wants what is best for me. How grateful I am for this beautiful force (spirit).

MEDITATION FOR TODAY

Help me to not forget how accepting and loving You are.

TODAY I WILL REMEMBER

God loves me!

March 14

REFLECTION FOR TODAY

When I concentrate too hard on what I want out of life, I lose track of what God wants. But when I concentrate on living as I think God wants me to, listening to my heart and being ready to accept with good humor that which I cannot change, I almost always get from life something better than I could have asked for. I still have a tendency to say, "Please, God, let me have this or do that," but I almost always add, "if it be Your will." And I mean it!

MEDITATION FOR TODAY

Remind me when I am demanding that if I surrender, I will get more than I asked for.

TODAY I WILL REMEMBER

I will try to get out of my own way and trust God to handle what I cannot.

March 15

REFLECTION FOR TODAY

We struggled through many days depending on things or people to make us happy. Yet nothing outside us could give us that feeling of security and happiness we sought. Finally, in desperation, we reached out, honestly. Being vulnerable, we began to gain what we had sought from the external. At first we were quite surprised to find we could create happiness and belonging by our own efforts. The more we risk being open, the more we are given.

MEDITATION FOR TODAY

Because honesty brings me a sense of security, help me to be willing to risk being vulnerable.

TODAY I WILL REMEMBER

Being vulnerable brings us much of what we need.

March 16

Just as it takes me time to think out the right decision to make and the right course of action to take using EA principles, I must learn to allow others time to make the right decisions too. I am not going to react to life any more; I am going to act - maturely, kindly, considerately. The slights I feel can very often be explained away by looking at things from another view - the other person's. Sometimes if I just wait patiently, people may want to change their minds or maybe ask questions.

MEDITATION FOR TODAY

Remind me that things are not always black and white; more often grey.

TODAY I WILL REMEMBER

The best decisions for me are not always to walk away from people or problems.

March 17

REFLECTION FOR TODAY

This day is often spent in celebrations of all kinds by those people of Irish heritage and many others who are Irish only for the day. My memories evoke many boisterous parties that ended disasterously. Anger and bitterness spilled over among friends and relatives. Like other holidays, when spent alone, it can be traumatic. Since working on my life with the Twelve Steps, I have found it is possible to celebrate sanely - to be with loving, understanding friends and to have fun without the emotional upheavals of the past. I have to be willing to reach out to all caring people of all races and say, "Let's be Irish together today."

MEDITATION FOR TODAY

Help me remember that holidays can be good days if I celebrate wisely as the Program teaches me. Do not ever let me dread another "special" day.

TODAY I WILL REMEMBER

I cannot be a parade by myself.

March 18

REFLECTION FOR TODAY

How we talk to ourselves creates how we ultimately feel. How often we tell ourselves that we are awful, something that happened is terrible, or we should be different or the circumstances should be different. Yet we are the way we are and life is the way it is. Acceptance of ourselves as we are and life as it is does not come easily. Again and again we struggle to be something we are not and to make things outside ourselves different from what they are. We use valuable energy and feel no better for the effort we invested.

MEDITATION FOR TODAY

May I talk about myself and life in ways which are accepting. The gift I will receive is peace.

TODAY I WILL REMEMBER

I will be aware of how I talk to myself.

March 19

REFLECTION FOR TODAY

As an adult I am just beginning to appreciate the child in myself. The ability to be a child is the willingness to trust to be vulnerable, to risk being laughed at or criticized. Although being vulnerable can be frightening, being vulnerable is also freeing. In becoming childlike, we gain the ability to play and to respond to life with laughter and humor. Not always being concerned about what others are thinking of me is one of the greatest freedoms the Program gives me.

MEDITATION FOR TODAY

May I have a greater appreciation of the child inside of me for I now know that is the part of me which is willing to trust. I need to trust if I wish to become open to myself and to life.

TODAY I WILL REMEMBER

I will continue to risk letting the child in me out.

March 20

REFLECTION FOR TODAY

One of the features of emotional illness is repression and suppression of emotions. Feelings are considered bad or wrong and willpower is used to deny and avoid these feelings. This leads to an increasing load of emotional pain and confusion. Identifying and releasing feelings is one of the essential first steps to recovery of emotional health. Feelings are neither good nor bad and not to be judged and condemned. They are to be appropriately experienced and expressed. I need not feel guilty about the way I feel. I am responsible for making the decision to accept my feelings and manage them appropriately. Will I be a friend to my feelings today?

MEDITATION FOR TODAY

God, please help me let You guide me and strengthen me as I live a new emotional way of life.

TODAY I WILL REMEMBER

Acceptance, experience, and expression — not condemnation, repression, and suppression.

March 21

A person who continues to run from pain ultimately finds he or she has to deal with some type of neurosis: depression, anxiety, or some other obsessive or compulsive behavior. Only when my pain became so great did I stop running. Then I had to deal with both the pain my neurosis created plus the original pain I had run from in the first place. Once I learned I was creating more pain by running, I became more willing to face myself honestly on a daily basis. As I deal with my pain I keep from developing another type of neurosis.

MEDITATION FOR TODAY

If I begin to run, God, slow me for I know You do not want me to hurt myself any more.

TODAY I WILL REMEMBER

As I face my pain, I learn about myself and my pain turns into a gain.

March 22

When I first started to work the Twelve Steps, I felt when I got to Step Twelve my life would be manageable and I would not be powerless. I did get to Twelve and many parts of my life became manageable, but I am still as powerless as when I first started. My *Higher Power* is making today manageable, not *my* power. The word manage means to control, to take charge of, to succeed in accomplishing. Am I willing to admit I can't control, take charge of, or succeed in life by myself? To admit I am powerless over my emotions is one thing, but to admit I can't manage my own life does sound hopeless and helpless. But there is help and hope with a Higher Power as my manager.

MEDITATION FOR TODAY

Help me to see what areas of my life I am still trying to manage and help me turn them over to You.

TODAY I WILL REMEMBER

My Higher Power is a better manager than I am.

March 23

Step Four suggests honesty with myself. Self-deception multiplies my problems and is an obstacle to the resolution of many of them. A searching and fearless moral inventory of my irrational behaviors and negative attitudes, like surgery for an inflamed appendix, is essential in my search for better emotional health. Self-justification may tempt me to explain away each fault as I uncover it. I may blame the shortcomings of others to excuse my own. On the other hand, lack of God-given humility may be clouding my appreciation and realization of my true value and worth. I have both weaknesses and strengths.

MEDITATION FOR TODAY

Remind me that my strength grows day by day when I face myself as I am and patiently correct whatever is keeping me from growing into the person I want to be.

TODAY I WILL REMEMBER

I will find serenity and stability only when I am honest with myself.

March 24

REFLECTION FOR TODAY

After working Steps One, Two and Three, it is tempting to sit back and say, "Okay, I'll let go; You take over." This does not work. It is like having a well and saying, "Why am I thirsty?" A well has clear, cool, refreshing water but the water must be pumped or drawn out. We must use our faith to do what we know is right. We must seek counsel, meditate, and work on the Steps. In any case, this Program does not call for giving up; it calls for surrender. We are endowed with unique qualities which can be used to make our life and the lives of others better. Part of faith is seeking these qualities and using them when we find them. The love and acceptance of the Program is the oil and fuel of the pump which will draw this faith and these qualities up into the light for us.

MEDITATION FOR TODAY

I pray I may use my faith in order that I may grow.

TODAY I WILL REMEMBER

Faith is like a deep well. It has great potential but is worthless if not used.

March 25

REFLECTION FOR TODAY

It is still too easy for me to get down. Not way down into deep depression, but down enough to make me work to get up. If I stay even a little bit down for long, I know how easy it is to slide further and further in that direction. It has been a long time since I have been really depressed, but because of the pain it caused me, the fear of depression is always there. When the down feeling hits, it is time to act "as if" and start thinking positive thoughts. I must concentrate on the good in my life and the good in me. I must turn off the "feel sorry for yourself" ballads and tune in to humor which helps my day become increasingly better.

MEDITATION FOR TODAY

Let me always be aware of any downward trend in my thinking. Give me the strength to turn my thoughts to the positive.

TODAY I WILL REMEMBER

Today is an up day.

March 26

As I look back over my life, I realize there were many times when I "blew" it. I was trying too hard and never quite made it. I finally realized that by myself and my own power I could not accomplish what I needed to make me happy. Now I am learning to surrender to my Higher Power and recognize my need for help and a program to really live a full life. I don't need to defend myself continuously because when I turn things over to my Higher Power, I am no longer responsible for the results; only for the efforts expended.

MEDITATION FOR TODAY

May I be receptive to the good You have in store for me this day and every day.

TODAY I WILL REMEMBER

My control led to unhappiness so for today I will give my Higher Power a chance.

March 27

A friend once put a tomato plant in a window box and placed it under plastic outside an open window during the fall. It continued to bear fruit well past the normal time, but the fruits became successively smaller. This is like us. We try to avoid our dormant times by continuing intense activity when we need quiet "non-productive" time. Our efficiency slides. We become tired and tense. Basically we waste ourselves. Sometimes it is hard to say no. It is difficult to keep inner space high enough on our priority list.

MEDITATION FOR TODAY

May I take time off as I need it, realizing this is essential to my ability to produce and even cope.

TODAY I WILL REMEMBER

I need "a quiet time of meditation".

March 28

REFLECTION FOR TODAY

Most of us long to be known and understood in depth, yet we resist this self-disclosure for with it comes a fear of loss. We may fear: What if my loved one dies? Or walks away? How will I survive? The loss won't be so great and won't hurt so much if I don't care so much. Often we are unaware that after intimate moments we create distance by becoming bored, irritated, or angry because we don't want to lose the feeling of being in control of our lives. We can be assured our fear of intimacy is normal, yet hurtful if we allow it to control us.

MEDITATION FOR TODAY

May I be reminded that unless I risk the loss, I will remain lonely and empty in the present moment.

TODAY I WILL REMEMBER

To let someone love me, I need to be vulnerable. To be vulnerable, I have to let go of control. I will resist closing up or running away.

March 29

REFLECTION FOR TODAY

There have been a handful of very special people who have come into my life. These people have been instruments of a great deal of healing. For someone who had tried to be as self-sufficient as I had, accepting their help was tough. When I became aware that not to accept their care and support would be very self-defeating, it became easier to reach out. As I have been able to let go of pride and fear and reach out, I learned more and more about my own inner beauty.

MEDITATION FOR TODAY

Nudge me, Higher Power, if I try to become self-sufficient once again. It is so lonely behind that wall.

TODAY I WILL REMEMBER

By letting love in, I have found myself and a caring Higher Power.

March 30

When I am troubled with my character defects of impatience or perfectionism, I can reflect on the Slogan "Easy Does It." When I plant seeds in my garden, I do not go and dig them up every day to see how fast they are growing. Similarly, when I plant myself in my EA chapter, nourished by the experience, strength, and hope of my fellow members, I can allow myself the fullness of time for growth, expressed in small daily increments.

MEDITATION FOR TODAY

May I not overreach myself and be content with my natural rate of growth.

TODAY I WILL REMEMBER

I am nurtured by the fertile garden (my group), and warmed by the sunlight of the spirit (my Higher Power). I will bloom in my own way, in my own time.

March 31

Choices are not always easy. I do have a choice when a decision is called for. I may not recognize the choices and often say, "I had no choice but to..." and so on. But the actual situation may have been that the alternative to what I chose was so undesirable I did not give it any rank. For example, I am learning that I always have the choice of not choosing. In other words, I can ignore the situation. And I have realized that is making a choice. I recently heard the idea, "Not to choose is to choose." Hopefully the idea will help me learn to evaluate all alternatives more thoroughly.

MEDITATION FOR TODAY

Help me to be honest with myself and my situation. May I think about that the next time I feel short on choices.

TODAY I WILL REMEMBER

Choices are almost always available.

April

April 1

Guilt comes from violating our own or significant other's values. Guilt says, "I made a mistake, I can ask forgiveness." Shame comes from an attitude or feeling of falling short, being inadequate, worthless and helpless. We can recognize shame by such thoughts as: How can anyone like me? I am sicker than others; I am a bad person. Shame is our biggest obstacle to growth because it is tied to our being. Certainly we cannot get rid of our being by asking forgiveness. Yet shame must be dealt with. As we betray our shame, we can begin to accept our human limitations.

MEDITATION FOR TODAY

Let me be aware today of how I speak to myself. Remind me that I am loveable.

TODAY I WILL REMEMBER

Guilt says, "I made a mistake." Shame says, "I am a mistake."

April 2

REFLECTION FOR TODAY

One of the toughest things I ever have to do is get myself going after a setback. The fear of ridicule and the heartbreak of disappointment sap me of the drive and energy needed to start up again. First I need to ask my Higher Power for a bold dash of enthusiasm to set up a spark of hope which is a driving force that enables me to try again. Upsets, setbacks, and unsuccessful attempts can become ways for me to strengthen my emotional stability by reexamining my priorities. If my method did not work, why not? I have to take a new look at the problem by viewing it from someone else's standpoint and by detaching myself. Maybe I cannot see the forest for the trees. I can try again with the help of my Higher Power grasping one hand and the EA Program and friends clinging tightly to the other.

MEDITATION FOR TODAY

Give me back my enthusiasm and hope when at first I do not succeed.

TODAY I WILL REMEMBER

My success is measured by my willingness to keep trying.

April 3

Perfectionism is one of my character defects. When I worked hard and honestly on my Fourth Step, I was anticipating a feeling of happiness and accomplishment. I had already made plans to share it with my Fifth Step person. The day came and my strong feelings were: "It's not good enough; it doesn't mean anything; the work was less than adequate." I reviewed my Fourth Step and realized not only was I looking for perfection, I was also fearful of rejection. Only with that trust in my Higher Power and knowledge that I had honestly tried to do a good job could I overcome the fear and share my Fourth Step.

MEDITATION FOR TODAY

Thank You for the strength and love and courage You give me whenever I ask for it.

TODAY I WILL REMEMBER

My Higher Power is always there for me.

April 4

REFLECTION FOR TODAY

Often we do not risk asking for something we want or need. We do not like being open about what is really important and possibly feeling rejected. If someone says, "No," it hurts; it may feel like rejection. It may be necessary to think differently about our response to someone who says, "No." That person may not be rejecting us after all but is simply unable to give what we are asking. I will think of several things I want and risk asking for them. I will be aware that if the person cannot give what I ask, it does not mean I am unworthy of my request.

MEDITATION FOR TODAY

God, remind me if I ask for ten things and receive only two, I have at least gained something.

TODAY I WILL REMEMBER

Risk nothing; gain nothing.

April 5

REFLECTION FOR TODAY

As I continue to take personal inventory as suggested in the Tenth Step, I become more aware as time passes of my wrongdoings as they occur. My being aware of these wrongs (gossip, irritability, selfishness, false pride, etc.) will not erase them from my life. Admitting and accepting them is a beginning. Realizing how they alienate me from myself as well as others can give me the incentive to give them up.

MEDITATION FOR TODAY

I ask for help from my Higher Power in handling each of my shortcomings.

TODAY I WILL REMEMBER

I will not only take my personal inventory, but also ask God to help me today to turn my defects into positive actions.

April 6

REFLECTION FOR TODAY

I am complex; my emotions do not have to make sense; they just are. As I accept them, contradictions and all, I can choose how I want to act. When I deny their existence or try to force them into my current understanding of my pattern, they control my actions. I become angry when there is no reason; I become depressed over nothing. As I accept myself, I find things make a lot more sense. This understanding usually comes without my exerting an intense effort. It most often "occurs" to me. This comes because, as I can accept all of me, I am open.

MEDITATION FOR TODAY

Help me to remember my future growth is unlimited.

TODAY I WILL REMEMBER

Today I can accept.

April 7

REFLECTION FOR TODAY

All I have are these twenty-four hours. Each second, minute, and hour I have a choice. Do I realize how many choices I do make each day however small they are? I am responsible when I am making decisions. Each choice I make helps me to grow. Some decisions I make might be right, some might be wrong, but I grow from all of them. I gain more confidence with each decision I make.

MEDITATION FOR TODAY

Give me the courage to make decisions.

TODAY I WILL REMEMBER

The worst choice is to make no choice but even that is a choice.

April 8

REFLECTION FOR TODAY

There seems to be a lot of contention about the concept of a Higher Power. Many easily accept the idea. Others find difficulty with it and blame their inability to acknowledge a Higher Power on what they perceive as logic. When we apply this to Step Two we can see that no matter how we try to define our understanding of our Higher Power we will come to a point where our concept does not make any sense. This we cannot change. Can I accept my Higher Power on its own terms, even though my Higher Power eludes logic?

MEDITATION FOR TODAY

To You whom I call my Higher Power, help me to believe You can restore balance to my life. Help me to avoid shading my understanding of You by molding You to my own ability to perceive.

TODAY I WILL REMEMBER

To logic, the Higher Power is profound.

April 9

REFLECTION FOR TODAY

The word surrender was never a part of my vocabulary. It meant weakness or quitting or being cowardly. It frightened me when I heard people at meetings say, "You have to surrender." I had to unlearn what had been instilled in me since childhood. I had to get rid of the old "never give up" adage that was so much a part of my life. It was extremely difficult to change that part of my background. But what a relief to not have to be responsible for the whole world and all its inhabitants any more. What a great comfort to be able to let go.

MEDITATION FOR TODAY

Help me to surrender my whole being to You daily.

TODAY I WILL REMEMBER

Surrender is serenity.

April 10

REFLECTION FOR TODAY

Secrets create a wall which keeps us lonely and isolated. They can also keep us from experiencing love. The more secrets I carried, the more shame I felt. The more shame I experienced, the more I wanted to close myself off from others. No longer do I have to alienate myself from others. There are people who are waiting and willing to listen to my secrets. They will not shame me. Instead they will understand because they have dealt with their own shame. By sharing my secrets I gain acceptance, belonging, and trust in my value as a person.

MEDITATION FOR TODAY

May I have the courage to share the secrets I have tried to keep buried in my subconscious for I realize this will set me free.

TODAY I WILL REMEMBER

By sharing my shame I can join the human race.

April 11

REFLECTION FOR TODAY

Step Eleven warns us to be careful of wishful thinking and rationalizing and to be conscious of what we may mistakenly believe to be divine guidance. Talking things out with someone else is suggested so we may gain perspective and understanding before we act. God most often speaks to us through other people. When we draw closer to the God of our understanding, we may be tempted to put aside people and rely only on our Higher Power. If we withdraw from human relationships thinking we are divinely inspired, we will once again find ourselves becoming self-righteous.

MEDITATION FOR TODAY

May I remain humble enough to recognize my need to continue to reach out to people.

TODAY I WILL REMEMBER

My relationship with God must be balanced with my relationship with people.

April 12

When I clean a drawer, I do not just rearrange the mess inside. I dump out the contents, throw away the things which are no longer useable, and keep only that which is valuable. I need to "dump" myself out to my Higher Power, throw away attitudes and behavior that have been hindering my relationships, and keep only those ideas which build and strengthen me.

MEDITATION FOR TODAY

Grant me the courage to take an honest look at myself.

TODAY I WILL REMEMBER

I trust that my Higher Power will help me know what to throw and what to keep.

April 13

REFLECTION FOR TODAY

I came into EA afraid - afraid of the past, present, and future, afraid of people, even those people who love me and whom I love. And afraid of being hurt again. EA has taught me that the opposite of fear is faith. As I learn to trust people, I trust my Higher Power and my fears lessen. Trust in people, trust in my Higher Power, and trust in myself go hand-in-hand.

MEDITATION FOR TODAY

May I remember that as I trust others, my Higher Power, and myself, my faith grows.

TODAY I WILL REMEMBER

Faith challenges fear.

April 14

Freedom can mean the ability to say, "No" to unproductive habits and unsatisfying ways of living. Freedom means surrendering my powerlessness to my Higher Power. It enables me to turn loved ones and troubles over to God's care. Freedom gives me the strength to say no when I want to and need to say no. Freedom can mean to be in control of what I do with my thoughts, feelings, and reactions. In the same way, freedom allows me to say yes to positive and productive attitudes. In other words, I am free to be the best me I can be.

MEDITATION FOR TODAY

Thank You for my freedom, which can be another word for self-discipline.

TODAY I WILL REMEMBER

Only the disciplined are free.

April 15

I came into this Program to learn more about myself and about the emotions I had hidden and repressed. Fear kept me from thinking rationally and from making decisions and acting in a way which was true to myself. It prevented me from setting any priorities in my life. When I acted out of fear, I hurt my self-image. Fear kept me from reaching out and letting others get close to me. It did not allow others to see the truly unique person I am.

MEDITATION FOR TODAY
Thank You for the freedom to grow.

TODAY I WILL REMEMBER
Trust!

April 16

REFLECTION FOR TODAY

I was addicted to fantasizing. For days I would be intoxicated by this fantasizing. I robbed myself of today, of myself, and other people. Some of my common escapes were: sleeping, drugs, alcohol, reading, and TV. They kept me away from people and I learned that I need people. Why did I try to escape from people? Because of fear of rejection and of the unknown.

MEDITATION FOR TODAY

Give me strength to live in today and to continue to reach out to people.

TODAY I WILL REMEMBER

What I am is real. I cannot escape from the reality that is me.

April 17

Our thoughts are like the environment. They started out clean and beautiful. Over the years we dump a lot of garbage into our minds. Some things decay over time (are biodegradable), while other things last forever and leave a garbage dump. The biodegradable refuse is excellent fertilizer — we learn from our mistakes. The plastic and metal must be disposed of — resentments, hate, envy, greed, etc. Just like the environment, there is a need for a one time wholesale cleanup once the situation is realized to be bad. Occasionally a new pocket will also need substantial work as new ground is covered. Those areas which have been cleaned will need continued policing to make sure they are actually clean and that there is no new build up.

MEDITATION FOR TODAY

Help me to be aware of the location of the garbage dumps in my life so I can pick and sort the fertilizer from the junk. Help me learn from the past and get rid of the things which are getting in the way of my recovery.

TODAY I WILL REMEMBER

Not all garbage is useless, nor is all that we are keeping useful.

April 18

REFLECTION FOR TODAY

There were many times before the Program when I did not know what to do next so I tried to do everything at once. I ended up filled with anxiety and accomplished nothing except to make an already upsetting situation worse. Am I looking at priorities today, sorting them out, handling only the things I can, and leaving the rest to God?

MEDITATION FOR TODAY

I ask for Your help to do all I can reasonably do today. Help me to: stop, relax, wait, have patience, and be aware during times of trouble that You will continue to care for me as You did when things were going well.

TODAY I WILL REMEMBER

I will do the best I can no matter what comes and leave the rest to God.

April 19

Meditation is not a job if by job we mean work done to deserve a reward. Meditation is a free gift of our Higher Power and is also the act of accepting that gift without questioning whether we deserve it or not. It is like an EA meeting inside ourselves wherein our Higher Power says, "I do not care where you have been or what you have done. I am glad you are here and I love you right now just as you are. You are precious to me no matter what."

MEDITATION FOR TODAY

You are always ready to give me the gift of Yourself. All I have to do is come to a meeting with You. Fear of not deserving Your unconditional love is often all that stands between You and me.

TODAY I WILL REMEMBER

I am deserving of unconditional love.

April 20

REFLECTION FOR TODAY

My "day", my "time" here on earth is part of God's plan for me. When things are following the natural flow, all seems to go well. How many times, through what I once termed coincidence, were the plans for the day changed for the better? I can stay out of trouble and accept whatever comes when I remember who is in charge of my life. My Senior Partner quite often has different and better ideas of how my day will unfold.

MEDITATION FOR TODAY

May I trust that Your plans for my day will be just what I need.

TODAY I WILL REMEMBER

I will rely on my God to get me through whatever this day brings.

April 21

Relating to another person intimately over an extended period of time is one of the most difficult things to do. We not only have to deal with our own problems, we have to deal with theirs, and our relationship. This increases the sources of potential problems considerably. It also increases the potential for growth and happiness. This is hard to see when in the midst of problems. If we can learn to relate while maintaining our individuality, we will have grown and found one of the keys to happiness and serenity. Often our partner or spouse will serve as a very clear mirror of ourselves. This can increase our awareness and acceptance so we can take action on those areas where we need work.

MEDITATION FOR TODAY

I pray I may be grateful for those around me who help me to see myself because they are aiding me in my recovery.

TODAY I WILL REMEMBER

Relationships, even those which cause pain, encourage us to grow.

April 22

When tense and confused, I need to realize I cannot force feed thoughts, positive or negative, to my hurting emotions. It only serves to cause more anxiety and depression. I must be accepting of my thoughts and feelings — be able to admit being unable to change them all at once or on my own. They may not make sense at the time and contradict what I believe. I need to accept them with gentleness and compassion for the disease was nurtured over a long period of time.

MEDITATION FOR TODAY

Help me accept that I am hurting and the emotions which follow. Help me to be gentle with myself and to reach out.

TODAY I WILL REMEMBER

Part of growth is realizing hurt people hurt people. I will apply this to myself.

April 23

REFLECTION FOR TODAY

I neither liked nor accepted most of my feelings. I either denied them or suppressed them. This denial and suppression caused my symptoms of anxiety, panic, insomnia, depression, etc. Feelings always come out somewhere. By willpower alone I have never been able to stop feeling what I did not wish to feel. Only to the degree that I accept my feelings can I surrender them to a Higher Power. Only in this process will the feelings be free to change. Many times I find myself with a feeling I do not want and I try to talk it away without accepting it. That is when I get locked into the feeling I want to be rid of. I must go back to Step One for powerlessness, Step Two for believing in a Higher Power, and Step Three for surrender.

MEDITATION FOR TODAY

Help me to accept my feelings and then surrender them to You. Remind me that if they are not changed quickly, it might be I need to learn something from what I am experiencing.

TODAY I WILL REMEMBER

Feelings can only change when they are accepted and surrendered.

April 24

REFLECTION FOR TODAY

Today will be a GREAT day. I believe it in my mind, my heart, and my bones. Only good things will happen to me and for me. It may rain, snow, or sleet, but so what? My inner sun will be shining. As I smile, "good morning" at others, they will feel better and pass on the smile to someone else, thus creating a network of smiles. Though the circumstances of each individual's day may be different, there is one similarity for all of us. We have the choice to think positive thoughts. I choose today to believe that this day will be great. These thoughts are contagious and can work as rapidly as virus germs.

MEDITATION FOR TODAY

Help me to be a carrier of positive attitudes. May I always realize that happiness spreads happiness.

TODAY I WILL REMEMBER

No antibiotic can "cure" positive or happy thoughts and actions.

April 25

REFLECTION FOR TODAY

What a joyous feeling when I realize it is never too late to begin again. There is never a time when it is too late for me to start all over. How delightful to know this day can be my turning point — the beginning of a whole new way of life. It is never too late to turn to my Higher Power, who patiently waits for me. It is never too soon to surrender my burdens and to enter into a more spiritual life. It is never too late for me to make amends, to forgive, and to forget. If I need to correct things, it is never too late to do so.

MEDITATION FOR TODAY

Thank You, God, for the knowledge that I can always start over without any shame.

TODAY I WILL REMEMBER

It is never too late.

April 26

In the aftermath of inventorying my specific defects of character, I found that underlying them all was a profound conviction that I am fundamentally defective in my very being. I am programmed with these false instructions: "You are not good enough! And it is your fault. And you are responsible for being better. But no matter what you do you are weak and wrong, and you are condemned!" But in my Fifth Step my Higher Power gave me permission to accept myself for being me.

MEDITATION FOR TODAY

May I understand that I am not guilty for being no better than I am.

TODAY I WILL REMEMBER

I am a part — not apart.

April 27

If it seems that on page after page of this book you are told to let go and let God, it is because it is a lesson we all seem to need to learn over and over again. It sounds so simple. Why is it so hard to do and why do we continually need to be reminded? We need to be responsible for our lives, to do all that we can to solve our problems and deal with challenging situations, but we must remember that the responsibility is not ours alone. We may not know what our needs are, but our Higher Power does. We have someone to turn to for help at all times. We may think there is no way a certain situation can be resolved, but there is one who does know how it can be resolved.

MEDITATION FOR TODAY

May I remember that letting go does not mean I do not have to make any effort.

TODAY I WILL REMEMBER

Let God do the worrying.

April 28

I used to see God responding to me with a clenched fist. Of course this vision created fear and guilt and made me want to hide. Day by day my vision of my Higher Power has changed. The hand is no longer clenched, but open very wide. The arms are a place where I can retreat for comfort and security. God always guides my footsteps and, in the painful times when I stumble and fall, God will carry me until I can walk again.

MEDITATION FOR TODAY

Thank You, Creator, for the knowledge that You are with me always guiding my path. When I am hurting, may I remember I can look to You for comfort.

TODAY I WILL REMEMBER

God did not change; only my vision of God changed.

April 29

REFLECTION FOR TODAY

My happiness does not depend on anyone but me. It is not given to me by others; nor can I earn it from others. Whether I am happy or not is the result of my own attitude toward myself and toward shared experiences. I place a terrific burden upon others if I make them responsible for my happiness. In expecting too much from others, I alienate them and become frustrated and angry with myself and them. This can give me the feeling of loneliness while in the midst of a crowd.

MEDITATION FOR TODAY

Help me to search inward sufficiently so I can be my own best friend.

TODAY I WILL REMEMBER

My happiness comes from a positive appreciation of myself.

April 30

REFLECTION FOR TODAY

"Turning it over" to my Higher Power is an exercise in accepting my limitations and a way of facing reality. I am saying, "This is too big for me; I am too weak and it overwhelms me." I am letting go of a struggle which, in most cases, I could not hope to win. I am acknowledging there are some things too complicated, too difficult, and perhaps even too abstract for me to deal with at this moment. Maybe later, when I am able to break a big problem into little bits and pieces, I will once again take up the challenge. But not now. Not while it is bigger than I am.

MEDITATION FOR TODAY

May I learn to live a manageable life by tackling manageable problems, and turning the rest over. May I comfortably accept my limitations.

TODAY I WILL REMEMBER

Today I will pick on problems my own size.

May

May 1

REFLECTION FOR TODAY

People need to be able to protect themselves without doing damage to others. I can learn to protect my sense of well being without injuring someone else's. Whenever I have to say no, tell someone I do not like something they are doing, tell someone when I am hurting, and ask for or allow my own needs to be met, I need to do it without putting anyone else down. I need to deal with the issue - not the personality - and yet take responsibility for myself by not blaming others.

MEDITATION FOR TODAY

Help me to know that if I am honest, I need not become defensive.

TODAY I WILL REMEMBER

To be assertive.

May 2

Spiritual awakenings are sometimes disguised as rude awakenings. Our expectations can become so overstated in our minds we lose sight of the goal of our life, happiness. Receiving life as it comes is the wisdom of the Serenity Prayer. Unmet expectations often bring anger. If we find ourselves hurt repeatedly, it is time to look at our priorities and our expectations realistically. Then our rude awakening becomes a spiritual awakening.

MEDITATION FOR TODAY

May I have the courage to look at my wants honestly and to change them if necessary.

TODAY I WILL REMEMBER

I will be grateful for rude awakenings.

May 3

REFLECTION FOR TODAY

Some of the friends I have made in the Program have become like members of a caring, nurturing family. When I can look across the room and see the sparkle in someone's eyes as they respond to me, I know without a doubt I am loved. The sense of belonging and being loved was something I always wanted desperately. I had felt like I was on the outside looking in. I was lonely even in a crowd. No longer do I have to feel alienation and loneliness for I have come home. I have found a place where I can be me.

MEDITATION FOR TODAY

Help me never to take for granted the wonderful and healing gift of friendship.

TODAY I WILL REMEMBER

If I am feeling lonely, I can reach out to a brother or sister in the fellowship.

May 4

REFLECTION FOR TODAY

Sometimes it is difficult to say, "Thank you." When the good life of EA becomes a habit, we express gratitude for the big miracles, but what about the little day-to-day "gifts from above?" One way which has worked for me with the people around me is for me to buy a box of inexpensive and decorative thank-you notes, or make my own. Then I give myself a time limit, two weeks or a month, to use up every note. This makes me even more aware of how God gives me gifts through other people because I am looking for them.

MEDITATION FOR TODAY

I ask for Your strength, guidance, and care. I thank You for everything which has been given to me today.

TODAY I WILL REMEMBER

I will not be afraid to say thank you.

May 5

REFLECTION FOR TODAY

The person in a relationship who is most open gains the most while the person who is least open has the most control. It is scary for most of us to risk being open and vulnerable. But each time we do so, we allow someone to truly know us. We open ourselves to the experience of feeling loved. We also learn about our capacity to love. The person who remains closed may feel in control but in control of what? That is only blocking the love needed to make a meaningful existence.

MEDITATION FOR TODAY

May I risk being open and gladly accept the gift of love.

TODAY I WILL REMEMBER

To be known is to be loved.

May 6

REFLECTION FOR TODAY

Once upon a time I thought I was a victim. People and circumstances had me caught and I was angry that no one came to rescue me. I know now that a power greater than myself can set me free any moment I am willing. If I am willing, God is able. People who I thought hated me, gossiped about me, ignored me, or scorned me had a hook in me. I let them control my feelings. I was surprised to discover I could remove that hook by including them in my prayers.

MEDITATION FOR TODAY

I pray for gentleness, generosity, and gratitude.

TODAY I WILL REMEMBER

I need never be a victim. God's power and my willingness make me a victor.

May 7

REFLECTION FOR TODAY

This day will bring new challenges. I shall be faced with situations which I may label as positive or negative. Since being in the Program, it is easier for me to handle the positive. In dealing with the negative, I need to act positive by reaching out to others through phone calls, meetings, people, and meditating. These are all things the Program teaches me to do and they work.

MEDITATION FOR TODAY

When things puzzle me and do not render themselves to an easy solution, help me to turn them over to You for special handling.

TODAY I WILL REMEMBER

What my mind cannot fathom can always be delegated to my Higher Power for proper disposition.

May 8

REFLECTION FOR TODAY

If I think I am perfect, then I cannot make mistakes. I either have to deny the mistakes I do make or blame them on someone else (difficult if the other person refuses to accept blame). Because I must do a thing perfectly or not at all, I am afraid to try something new. I might make mistakes while learning or I might make a fool of myself. I cannot be human if I insist on being perfect. Only humans can have fun by allowing themselves to appear foolish while making mistakes and learning from them.

MEDITATION FOR TODAY

May I remember the fun I missed trying to be perfect, and the energy I wasted holding back or trying too hard. May I not take myself so seriously.

TODAY I WILL REMEMBER

Only God is perfect. I am human; therefore, I will make mistakes.

May 9

REFLECTION FOR TODAY

Since being in the Program, I have often heard about acceptance. In the past I have assumed acceptance meant resigning myself to the fact there were many things I could not change or control; situations, people, and often even myself. Lately the word acceptance has taken on new meaning. I have come to understand that acceptance also means taking the gifts my Higher Power offers. These gifts: serenity, courage, wisdom, and love are freely given. My Higher Power puts these gifts before me every minute of my life. I need only accept them. Sometimes I am blind to them or refuse to believe they are really mine. I see strings attached when, in reality, I am being offered the gift of freedom. However, the gifts never stop being offered even when I reject them. No matter what I do or do not do, these gifts are never withdrawn. Acceptance means we can take these gifts which have always been and will always be meant for us.

MEDITATION FOR TODAY

May I accept all the gifts You so freely offer.

TODAY I WILL REMEMBER

Acceptance is the gift of love I can give myself today and every day.

May 10

REFLECTION FOR TODAY

I often did things for others to make me feel good about myself. The good feelings lasted only temporarily. What an exciting awareness to discover my good feelings could never last from only "doing". Good feelings had to come to me from just "being" as in BEING responsible for myself by sharing my feelings and asking for something I may need. Self-worth is actually a byproduct of my being honest about what is really going on inside of me and following the guidance which I now know comes from a Higher Power, who often works through people, and then taking the risk to do what I feel led to do.

MEDITATION FOR TODAY

Thank You, God, for this new understanding. If I forget and try to go back to get my self-worth from only doing, I trust You will give me a nudge to let me know I am headed down the wrong path.

TODAY I WILL REMEMBER

Self-worth comes from being honest and responsible.

May 11

REFLECTION FOR TODAY

One of my worst habits has been that of finding fault and criticizing others for what they do or do not do. I have learned that habits are changed by replacing the bad with the good. I know now that when I look for something to praise and appreciate in someone, I do not have the inclination to criticize. Finding fault is replaced with understanding, tolerance, love, and patience. Just as I know God made me and loves me as I am, I must remember God feels the same about the other person. There is always *something* good in every one. I need to recognize that good.

MEDITATION FOR TODAY

Remind me always to look for the spark of good in a person before I judge harshly.

TODAY I WILL REMEMBER

I hate to be criticized; so do others.

May 12

REFLECTION FOR TODAY

The Program teaches us that when we turn our will and our life over to a Higher Power, that Higher Power will guide our lives. But, I asked myself, how will I know what to do? What is my Higher Power's responsibility and what is mine? The insight came: turn it over. God will show me what to do and how to do it. In a meeting, during meditation, reading, or in conversation an answer or idea comes. Once God gives me direction, I need to take action.

MEDITATION FOR TODAY

May I remember that when You guide my life it goes smoother than when I try to control it myself.

TODAY I WILL REMEMBER

God knows better than I do what is best for me.

May 13

REFLECTION FOR TODAY

In reflecting on my childhood I see how fear affected me and helped form my decisions to be a good person, an approval seeker, and to put someone else in charge of my life - someone I saw as stronger than me. At first this was my parent; later it was my mate. Fear caused me to feel helpless, inadequate, and insecure. When I make someone else responsible for me, I have unrealistic expectations of those persons. They cannot possibly live up to them. I constantly set myself up for disappointment and hurt. I blame them when things go wrong. I may retaliate with anger or with emotional withdrawal. How much better for me to accept responsibility for my own happiness and to let go of expecting others to do for me what I need to do for myself.

MEDITATION FOR TODAY

May I realize that my strength must come from a power greater than myself, not from other human beings.

TODAY I WILL REMEMBER

Faith lets us face our fears.

May 14

REFLECTION FOR TODAY

I came into EA as a last resort and I wanted to
get well yesterday. I did not want to admit
powerlessness as I believed that other people
were to blame for the mess I was in. If I could
just get those other people to change I would be
okay. The Program taught me that I have no
power or authority to control or change anyone
but myself. That power derives from God - not
from me. The first change was in my attitude.
Step One meant that my powerlessness had to
become an essential part of my thinking, feeling,
and acting. I must stop trying to control the un-
controllable (other people) and start correcting
what I have the right to change (my own attitudes and actions).

MEDITATION FOR TODAY

May I accept my own powerlessness and ask for
and accept Your power.

TODAY I WILL REMEMBER

I cannot change anyone or anything but myself
and then only with the help of God.

May 15

REFLECTION FOR TODAY

Sometimes people tend to try and control others for their own needs. Even though I fell into the receiving end of this most of my life, I now have a choice in the matter. I can refuse to be controlled by others, if I do what is right for me without fear of repercussions or verbal abuse. I am stronger now and my courage to speak up on matters of principle comes from my Higher Power. I will not turn down this gift of courage because of fear of what others might think, say or do in retaliation.

MEDITATION FOR TODAY

May I realize that what others do or say is not necessarily an honest judgement of me as a person. Even if they meant it as such, I need only answer to You.

TODAY I WILL REMEMBER

I do not have to let others control me. I have the Twelve Steps to use as my guide, not the judgements of others.

May 16

REFLECTION FOR TODAY

What does it really mean when I say in Step Six, "Were entirely ready to have God remove all these defects of character?" It means: I have to stop struggling (remembering I admitted my powerlessness in Step One) and to put the responsibility for the removal of my character defects into the hands of God. Am I then supposed to just sit idly by, waiting, "twiddling my thumbs"? Certainly not. I have a responsibility, too. My part, however, is not to enter into the struggle again but to become increasingly aware of the reality and presence of God in my life. To prepare myself for this I have to spend some time each day alone with my Higher Power in quiet prayer and meditation. This daily discipline is *my* assignment.

MEDITATION FOR TODAY

May Your presence in my life become ever more real to me, and may I open myself daily to Your guidance.

TODAY I WILL REMEMBER

The struggle is not mine; I put it in God's hands. My part is to draw nearer to God.

May 17

REFLECTION FOR TODAY

In the Program I grow in awareness of my need for God and my need for people. I go to God for quiet times of prayer and meditation. This relationship sends me out to people. My relationship with people draws me back again to God. Because I am a dependent person, finding a balance did not come overnight. But the balance of God and others in my life now brings me moments of comfort, peace, belonging, and security. I have found a place which feels like home.

MEDITATION FOR TODAY

When I am uncertain about my direction, help me to reach out to You and then to others.

TODAY I WILL REMEMBER

I will reach out to God and I will reach out to a friend.

May 18

REFLECTION FOR TODAY

I am getting to be who I want to be. My own self was buried for so long I did not know who or what I was. The Program has taught me honesty which has enabled me to start knowing the real me. I no longer have the desperate need for approval from others. My own approval of me is more important. I am gaining a firm sense of self and a good feeling of confidence. I like the real me as I am. That does not mean I can't be better. It just means I can be satisfied with who I am right now as long as I keep trying for improvement.

MEDITATION FOR TODAY

Thank You, God, for helping me to learn that self-satisfaction is not the same as false pride.

TODAY I WILL REMEMBER

Today I am terrific!

May 19

REFLECTION FOR TODAY

Until I began to accept my dependency, I was unable to become independent in a healthy manner. As I struggled with my dependency, I came to accept the support and care I needed. I have matured and gained great freedom. Today I can accept that I am both dependent and needy, as well as being independent. This is what makes me human.

MEDITATION FOR TODAY

May I recognize my need for others yet not expect others to take care of me.

TODAY I WILL REMEMBER

No one can do for me what I need to do for myself, but I need others to encourage me and support my efforts.

May 20

REFLECTION FOR TODAY

Our mind is so powerful in its ability to rationalize. It can make us believe the truth is a lie and what is false is reality. As we recognize how we so often delude ourselves with our thinking, we see how necessary it is now to have friends with whom we are able to share anything. We have suffered enough from our self-defeating behavior. We do not deserve to keep hurting ourselves. Unless we unconsciously wish to continue suffering, we will be open and honest with someone.

MEDITATION FOR TODAY

May I not take action blindly. First I will share my plan with someone I trust.

TODAY I WILL REMEMBER

Openness and honesty are keys to acting responsibly.

May 21

How often have we expected 100% from a friend and felt disillusioned because that person could not meet our expectations? On the other hand, how many of us have a tendency to gravitate toward people who can only give 25% ? We may be so used to receiving only crumbs in our relationships we think that is all we deserve. Yet, as we grow, we discover we deserve to have people in our lives who can give us 90% - at least some of the time. In fact, to grow to our potential, we need a handful of friends who think we are terrific and wonderful - at least 75% of the time.

MEDITATION FOR TODAY

Higher Power, guide me to relationships which will help me realize my potential.

TODAY I WILL REMEMBER

I will seek relationships which value me, relationships on an equal level. In turn, I will value my friends.

May 22

REFLECTION FOR TODAY

There are times when my anger is enjoyable and almost fun - particularly when I feel I have been treated unfairly. I relish feeling sorry for myself and love to go over and over in my mind the grievances done to me. I perform a play mentally and plan the bitter confrontation soon to come. I play both roles and write the script for the wrongdoer and the "wrongee". I enjoy the taste of the words I'm going to use. I don't sleep well while I am rehearsing this mental play and soon I am angry with me and the whole world. That is when the fun stops. That is when the truth sets in. That is when I realize I am hurting only myself. The person I have lost sleep over has been sleeping soundly all the time. That is the time when I start praying for the person I am angry with.

MEDITATION FOR TODAY

Help me to plan at least a mental script which uses the words, "I forgive you."

TODAY I WILL REMEMBER

Anger is an emotion I cannot nurture; it costs me my serenity.

May 23

Comparing myself to others continues to be a well-established habit which does not diminish easily. I repeatedly fall into comparing "my insides" to the "outside" of others. I see the self-assurance others exhibit as a sign of their independence, self-reliance, and success and an indication they have no problems; therefore, I am unlike them. My self-pity and low self-esteem grow to gigantic extremes. I become silent and withdrawn or sarcastic and verbally abusive. In my "fighting back", I hurt others because I hurt. I do not look further. If I did, I would discover they, too, have an equal amount of problems with which they must cope, but they choose not to let their problems overwhelm them.

MEDITATION FOR TODAY

Please be with me and help me overcome my habit of comparing myself with others. Help me to see the good in myself as well as in others.

TODAY I WILL REMEMBER

I am only hurting myself when I compare myself to others.

May 24

REFLECTION FOR TODAY

I have finally realized that many of my depressions (not anywhere near the ruts and holes I used to dig myself into) are caused by my character defect of procrastination. I wait until the last moment to do all the things I have been planning to do for several months. When all fall due at the same time, it is not possible to accomplish all the goals and then I lay a guilt trip on myself. The guilt can be the beginning of the trip to depressionland. I am learning to keep my "job" list realistic and to do the best I can with it.

MEDITATION FOR TODAY

Remind me that procrastination can lead me one rut closer to my deep hole of depression.

TODAY I WILL REMEMBER

I will do at least one thing, whether big or small, from my "job" list today and be grateful I could accomplish something; there were many days in the past when I could not.

May 25

REFLECTION FOR TODAY

Each morning I place myself and all my worries and problems into God's loving care. I ask my Higher Power to take charge of my life for this day. I surrender my mind, my body, my life, and my will asking for the strength and courage which I need to keep going. I turn my family and friends over to God also, asking they be helped with their health, happiness, and any concerns they may have. When I have done this, I then ask for specific help with problems such as too little patience, intolerance, my habit of criticizing, and unforgiveness. This starts the day off on the right track for me.

MEDITATION FOR TODAY

Thank You, God, for being there so I can turn myself over to Your safekeeping.

TODAY I WILL REMEMBER

The day is easier when my concerns are in God's hands.

May 26

REFLECTION FOR TODAY

Sometimes I dwell on a problem which has no quick and easy answer. It might be a troubled relationship, a problem at work, sexual difficulties, physical pain, or any of a multitude of situations that cannot be fixed instantly to my liking. By remaining focused on a negative aspect of my life, I activate character defects such as self-pity, resentment, anger, and false guilt. When I accept the fact that life involves much problem solving and a necessary ingredient for sane living is the ability to peacefully endure until a solution is discovered, I am able to let go of the urgency of the problem facing me. By not tying up all my energies in the unpleasantness and hopelessness of a problem, I free myself to turn to my Higher Power for help in finding the right answer.

MEDITATION FOR TODAY

Help me to let go of my childish desire to have no problems, and to patiently trust that answers will unfold as I continue to work the Program.

TODAY I WILL REMEMBER

I *can* live at peace with unsolved problems.

May 27

REFLECTION FOR TODAY

My Higher Power gave me this body and the free will to use it or abuse it. Today I will bless my body and all the organs which are part of it. Bodies are true miracles. Picture your heart pumping fresh blood to your little toes and your lungs sending oxygen throughout. I thank God for every function and faculty of this priceless possession. Today I will treat my body as it should be treated with proper food, rest, exercise, and attention. I will clean it carefully and dress it in clean and appropriate garments. I thank God for the everyday healing which constantly renews and rebuilds the miracle of my body.

MEDITATION FOR TODAY

May my body continue to be healed and may I always treat it with respect.

TODAY I WILL REMEMBER

A healthy mind needs a healthy body.

May 28

REFLECTION FOR TODAY

It is hard to believe that self-discipline can mean freedom. In my old way of thinking discipline meant work, drudgery, a chore, or something to rebel against. But I have learned that disciplining my reactions, keeping my "cool", rolling with the punches, and living one day at a time has brought order to my chaotic life. Self-discipline gives me a sense of accomplishment, self-confidence, self-respect, and it frees me to go on to new endeavors.

MEDITATION FOR TODAY

Help me to discipline myself so I can be free to be me.

TODAY I WILL REMEMBER

I can do it.

May 29

REFLECTION FOR TODAY

Everyone needs a quiet place. A place to think, to pray, or dream where we can go to organize our thoughts and close out the clutter of the outside world. Many people take time in the morning when they get out of bed to meditate and receive the message which their Higher Power has for them. Many of us wait until the late evening when our families are asleep and the house is quiet. Some people often feel their regular weekly support meetings are a refuge where they can receive love, friendship, and emotional nourishment to strengthen them. A private talk and cup of coffee with a friend can also put things in perspective.

MEDITATION FOR TODAY

Help me find my quiet place.

TODAY I WILL REMEMBER

R & R: rest and recuperate; relax and repair; renew and recover.

May 30

This morning I do not feel so well. I feel stodgy and off-balance for no apparent reason. I just do not feel like being "spiritual". But I can go and sit down or slouch down and write about how I am feeling, about all of me, and open a window to my Higher Power. I know God is there with what I need. Why do I sometimes want to resist? Why do I say no to being open? It seems to take a lot of personal willfulness to oppose this resistance. That is why I feel so well when I say yes. I really am loveable.

MEDITATION FOR TODAY

Help me to stop resisting.

TODAY I WILL REMEMBER

My power comes in surrendering!

May 31

Suicide is the ultimate copout. It is the final giving up. It is DEATH which means life is over! No more goals, no more hopes, no more dreams. Maybe we feel that is what we want. Many of us have contemplated suicide; many more probably will. What held us back? For me it was the knowledge of what it would do to my family. My father and an aunt both committed suicide and I remembered what those experiences had done to me. No matter how hopeless my life was, and it was pretty bad, I could not leave my loved ones with those same feelings. As long as there is life, there is hope; an old cliche but still very true. Life can and will get better. Turn it over to your Higher Power and wait one more day.

MEDITATION FOR TODAY

Oh, God, never let me forget how I felt when my loved ones took their own lives.

TODAY I WILL REMEMBER

I CAN live this one day - one hour at a time.

June

June 1

REFLECTION FOR TODAY

Sometimes I forget that I am never alone and have a terrible feeling of deprivation because of absence of friends and loved ones. On those days I have to remind myself of God's presence within me. I have forgotten for that moment that God is always with me - at home, at work, in the car, or even in unfamiliar surroundings. Wherever I am, God is with me. When I remember that fact, a feeling of peace and serenity enfolds me and I relax. I feel strong, courageous, and loved. I can do all that is required of me this day. I can get along without the friends and loved ones until their return because my Higher Power is with me.

MEDITATION FOR TODAY

On lonely days, remind me of Your presence.

TODAY I WILL REMEMBER

God and I can conquer the world.

June 2

When battling with crippling emotions, it is so easy to run in different directions or to remain immobilized, unable to decide where to start. In this state of confusion, I am like a wheel stuck in the mud, going nowhere. The antidote to this indecisiveness is my daily program. By deciding how I will spend the time given to me today, I am placing my wheels on firm ground. The Slogan "First Things First" can help me determine the order my day should follow. Another saying, "How important is it?" can guide me in any uncertainty; either in planning my time or in handling interruptions.

MEDITATION FOR TODAY

Give me a push if my wheels get stuck.

TODAY I WILL REMEMBER

This day is a gift. How I use it determines how much I enjoy the gift.

June 3

REFLECTION FOR TODAY

There are so many things I cannot change! What other people say and do and feel is beyond my power just as is the weather, the passing of time, and my basic physical makeup. To wish otherwise is to waste my energy on a dead end. When I accept the things I cannot change, I free myself to recognize opportunities in every situation. For my own serenity, I will take what good I can from everything I encounter today and leave the rest.

MEDITATION FOR TODAY

When one door is locked to me, please guide me toward the door which is open.

TODAY I WILL REMEMBER

I will focus on accepting myself just as I am.

June 4

REFLECTION FOR TODAY

Letting someone love me seems such a simple thing but in my emotional turmoil I had to make it complex. I had to start asking why. Why would someone want me? What were they after? What is this going to cost me? I found it impossible to receive a natural, tolerating, caring, free-flowing acceptance from another person. My first experience in this area was EA. I was totally accepted with no strings attached. With the help of these great people, I learned to accept their love. I learned that love is not control or manipulation. Love is letting people be themselves and loving them that way.

MEDITATION FOR TODAY

Your love has no strings attached. Help me to love the same way.

TODAY I WILL REMEMBER

Allowing someone to love me will not make me less of a person but more of a human being.

June 5

REFLECTION FOR TODAY

Too often I agonize over a problem as if all solutions depend on me. I try to anticipate what to do and what to say. I seem to have to torment myself a while before I remember it is not all up to me. God can help me and is willing to do so but I have to ask. Often I "discover" the solution quite soon after I ask. How wonderful to have such a friend to rely on.

MEDITATION FOR TODAY

May I remember to ask for Your help *early* in a problem.

TODAY I WILL REMEMBER

My Higher Power is my constant and willing source of help.

June 6

REFLECTION FOR TODAY

As my emotional illness progressed, I was able to cope with less and less. My world became smaller and smaller until I was finally trapped inside a prison of my own devising. This was my emotional bottom. Now I am recovering. Now I can be more aware of this beautiful world, and not take for granted, or ignore, the many things provided by the God who I understand. I can bring new things into my life. I believe life is meant to be full, rich, and joyful.

MEDITATION FOR TODAY

May I find one new thing for which to thank You. Help me let gratitude crowd out envy, wanting, and resentment.

TODAY I WILL REMEMBER

To thank my Higher Power for what I discover in my search.

June 7

REFLECTION FOR TODAY

I know that when I plant seeds of positive thoughts, more positive thoughts bloom from the seeds. The same is true of negative thoughts. I have the freedom to choose which of these seeds will be planted in the garden of my mind today. I can choose whether I will be content and serene for this twenty-four hour period or whether I will be depressed and in pain. I can direct my energies into healthy or unhealthy attitudes. I can be creative and productive or idle and destructive. I have learned that negativity can destroy me so my choice is obvious.

MEDITATION FOR TODAY

Help me to weed out negativity.

TODAY I WILL REMEMBER

I will reap a harvest of serenity which comes from the positive thought seeds which I plant.

June 8

I used to think I had to make everything perfect for my children. If they were given too much homework, I felt I should say something to the teacher. If my child did not play as many innings in a baseball game as I thought he should, I figured it was my responsibility to let that coach know how unjust I thought he was and try to change him. I cannot make life perfect for my children or for me, for that matter. It helps to try and determine how important the situation is. There really are not that many cases I have discovered which are important. However, at the time I often think it is of the utmost importance. I cannot change the coach, I cannot change the teacher, and, in fact, there are really very few people I can change - probably no one but myself. I do not always know what is best, nor is it realistic to attempt to make things perfect.

MEDITATION FOR TODAY

Help me to give others permission to be different from me.

TODAY I WILL REMEMBER

My serenity comes from knowing it is okay if it is not my will.

June 9

Without the pain which comes to warn us of a physical ailment, we could die very quickly. If we refuse to recognize the warning signs of emotional pain, we may not necessarily die, but we will be less alive to abundant living. Each time I am willing to risk sharing my pain, I gain support and acceptance. This support and acceptance makes it easier to risk again. This risking brings me the gifts of healing and wholeness.

MEDITATION FOR TODAY

When I am in pain, may I develop the ability to see ahead to a fuller life.

TODAY I WILL REMEMBER

Pain tells me something needs to be changed.

June 10

REFLECTION FOR TODAY

As we begin to look more positively at where we are, we will discover that all of our painful moments, if faced, lead us to learn more about ourselves. Everything we experience has its value. How much do we learn when things are going well? Don't we just coast along? Only pain pushes us to risk or to challenge the things in ourselves which we need and want to change. As we become more in touch with our needs, our values, and our goals, we are pushed to a new adventure.

MEDITATION FOR TODAY

Remind me that pain is an opportunity for growth.

TODAY I WILL REMEMBER

Our pain, if faced, helps us to find balance in our lives; the balance of self, others, and purpose.

June 11

REFLECTION FOR TODAY

Most of us can relate to the feeling of being used. Have we ever looked behind our feelings of being used? Why did we continue putting ourselves in situations which left us feeling inadequate, angry, guilty, and shameful? Were we not really being pleasers? It is one thing as a child to do things which bring us approval, but as adults we have the freedom of choice. We are not at the mercy of others for our self-worth. If we remain people pleasers, it is our own choice.

MEDITATION FOR TODAY

If I feel used, may I remind myself I am responsible for what happens to me.

TODAY I WILL REMEMBER

No one can use me unless I allow it.

June 12

REFLECTION FOR TODAY

One of the biggest hurdles to staying well emotionally is self-pity. Self-pity breeds all kinds of "I" trouble. It is like being on center stage with the spotlight on ourselves. It is the minor injury we let drag on for a while so we can let more people share in our pain. It is the tough emotional time when we feel so sorry for ourselves that we cannot see the world around us. It is a fog because our "eyes" are focused on ourselves. Some times asking God to help us over a crisis is the hardest thing to do. The reason is that our prayers may be answered and then we have to go on again. We may have to change and we cannot feel sorry for ourselves any longer.

MEDITATION FOR TODAY

I pray that I may have a willing heart and that I will lean on Your strength and love.

TODAY I WILL REMEMBER

When we take our "eyes" off of ourselves and begin to focus them on others, our "I" trouble clears up.

June 13

REFLECTION FOR TODAY

The thought of changes in my life used to fill me with dread. I felt uncertain and insecure when I realized my old patterns would not be the same. Now the thought of change is exciting. My life would be so dull and uninteresting if I never tried a new way of doing things or never accepted a challenge. I could not grow if I did not step out with faith to do more and be more than I thought I could do or be. Challenges fill my life with excitement. Sometimes I cannot meet the challenge but I know new ones will keep coming which I probably can meet. There is a joy in anticipation of learning, feeling, and experiencing new ways of living and growing.

MEDITATION FOR TODAY

I know You are with me through every change and I expect, accept, and give thanks for the change.

TODAY I WILL REMEMBER

Life is for living and growing no matter what my age.

June 14

Our Higher Power allows all of us complete freedom to do whatever we want. Why then can't I give others the same opportunity? Am I playing God in their lives? No. I am performing even one step higher. I am forcing my will onto them. "Live and let live" tells me to let go of them to make their own choices. Just because something is not right for me does not mean it is not right for them. I need not condone the actions of others, but I must accept the person.

MEDITATION FOR TODAY

May I quit pulling strings to change others. Remind me that You are guiding those I love and even those I do not like so well.

TODAY I WILL REMEMBER

I am not responsible for the actions of anyone else.

June 15

REFLECTION FOR TODAY

In the past I was taught to believe I was being conceited, selfish, and shameless if I liked myself. I could have a good time but not give myself any credit. This attitude led to unacceptance of and dislike of myself. I must be free of this attitude if I am to have emotional health. My sanity depends upon acceptance and love for myself as I am. It is essential that I appreciate me; only then can I enjoy being me.

MEDITATION FOR TODAY

Help me to appreciate myself as I am.

TODAY I WILL REMEMBER

Not only is it okay for me to feel good about myself, it is necessary.

June 16

REFLECTION FOR TODAY

Today I shall pause and consider all the positive and wonderful circumstances of my life; free gifts from my Higher Power which are showered upon me. It is time to state my gratitude for these blessings. I am grateful for my health and for my life. I am grateful for the loving and lovely people in my life: family, friends, and co-workers. They contribute to my happiness and well-being. I am grateful for the beauty surrounding me: sun, sea, blue sky, (even rain), and flowers. I am grateful for my sense of humor which eases my way along life's path. I am grateful especially for the EA Program which has taught me about appreciation and gratitude, as well as a way of life.

MEDITATION FOR TODAY

Thank You, Higher Power, for all the blessings of my life. Help me always to remember gratitude.

TODAY I WILL REMEMBER

I am blessed with a good life!

June 17

REFLECTION FOR TODAY

My life was scrambled eggs! Since you cannot put scrambled eggs back together, the next best thing was what to do? HOW? *Honesty, Openness, and Willingness.* With HOW in my life my egg is still scrambled, but I can now cope and accept that scrambled eggs are good, too. HOW adds to my life and makes it better just as adding bacon, toast, and jelly makes the scrambled eggs more satisfying.

MEDITATION FOR TODAY

May I realize that I can live with unsolved problems.

TODAY I WILL REMEMBER

However the egg is prepared, it can be good!

June 18

REFLECTION FOR TODAY

Those of us who have been sexually abused as children tend to feel a lot of shame, fear, and rage. If we do not face these feelings, we will hang onto self-defeating behavior. When we are willing to face our shame, fear, and rage, we can start to heal. It may be scary and painful to face those experiences from our past, but the option of not facing that pain seems far worse. A painful existence by denial is comparable to living in a self-made hell.

MEDITATION FOR TODAY

God, please help me to trust at least one person today with my secret pain.

TODAY I WILL REMEMBER

I do not have to continue feeling guilt and shame for childhood experiences.

June 19

While I was working on a jigsaw puzzle, I became aware of how much my life has been like this puzzle. Some pieces of my life fit into other pieces with ease while some do not mesh at all. On reflection, I realize that when I surrender problems to my Higher Power, those pieces of my life go together easily. When I take over the controls, no matter how I push and tug, none of the pieces fit. When my negative emotions take over, the colors of the puzzle and the colors of my life do not blend. The puzzle could never be finished if I continued in that manner. When I relax and work with my brain instead of hostile feelings, the pieces seem to go together of their own volition - just like the parts of my life.

MEDITATION FOR TODAY

When I struggle and flounder, help me to remember how jigsaw puzzles get put together.

TODAY I WILL REMEMBER

To solve a puzzle of life, turn it over and relax.

June 20

REFLECTION FOR TODAY

When I hit my emotional bottom, my sense of humor was one of the blessings I lost. It seemed so strange to me to see other people laugh. What was so funny? My whole world had fallen apart. I was irritated by people who could laugh. I was jealous because I missed my old friend, humor. I was emotionally locked up. When I came to EA, I was pleased to read that a Program Promise was that my sense of humor would return.

MEDITATION FOR TODAY

Thank You for the gift of my returned laughter.

TODAY I WILL REMEMBER

Laughter is one of the keys which opens doors to serenity.

June 21

REFLECTION FOR TODAY

Sometimes I find myself totally engrossed in wondering what someone close to me is thinking, what that person is doing, or is going to do next. I ask myself questions like: "How can I help or change the situation?", "What if...?", "How will I handle the problem if...?" I suddenly realize I am wasting away my own time and causing turmoil within myself. All my thoughts will do nothing to help or change a situation so I must let go and wait to see what happens.

MEDITATION FOR TODAY

May I realize the time I spend thinking about a situation or person is a form of controlling and that my own sanity depends on turning it over to You.

TODAY I WILL REMEMBER

My thoughts cannot change another person or situation. I can change only *myself*!

June 22

In the past I often got so distracted I forgot what it was I had set out to do and ended up doing nothing. Then I spent the rest of the day blaming others for my problems and berating myself for losing sight of my goal. Am I learning to concentrate on the task at hand? Am I stopping to check the physical, spiritual, mental, and emotional attitudes which all help to keep my train of thought on the track? Am I setting reasonable goals and remembering "first things first"?

MEDITATION FOR TODAY

Help direct my day. Remind me to stop along the way to remember a Concept, a Step, a Slogan, or a Just for Today to keep me aware of You.

TODAY I WILL REMEMBER

I will attach my mind to the engine and not to the caboose.

June 23

Before becoming a part of the Program, I was selfish and inconsiderate. There were so many times I said, "me first." I manipulated and maneuvered others into doing what I thought was right. Selfishly I demanded that everyone else do what I wanted. If they didn't, I sulked and I stormed. If that didn't work, I developed a headache or a mysterious pain to get the attention I thought I needed or deserved. I am trying today to be more considerate of others, more aware of their needs.

MEDITATION FOR TODAY

Although I know I need to take care of myself, help me to be considerate of others' needs.

TODAY I WILL REMEMBER

I'm important; others are too.

June 24

REFLECTION FOR TODAY

In dealing with many people and situations in my life, I find I feel I must hide the true me. Sometimes my emotions (especially fear) get in the way of my relating to other people and I feel I do not fit in. But there is hope! At an EA meeting I can be myself. I can share my feelings and show my emotions. I can be me. As I find strength through EA meetings and friends, I find this strength beginning to carry over in other areas of my life.

MEDITATION FOR TODAY

May I always remember that being emotional is not bad and does not make me weak. My emotions are given to me by You as a way to express all my inward feelings.

TODAY I WILL REMEMBER

I will love and accept me as I am.

June 25

REFLECTION FOR TODAY

I will not compare myself to others. In comparing, I become so preoccupied with the effect I produce and what others think of me that I forget who I am. I envy their talents so much I neglect to appreciate and develop my own. God creates only one of a kind and chooses the length of time each of us needs to gain insight and understanding. The insight God gives each of one of us will be different because WE are different.

MEDITATION FOR TODAY

May my Higher Power help me stop playing games with my personality and see my character defects so I can change my negative aspects into positive ones.

TODAY I WILL REMEMBER

Don't compare.

June 26

REFLECTION FOR TODAY

Whenever I pray for God's will for me, I must understand that as I move throughout this day I am probably doing what I should be doing. I was afraid that God's will for me would be something outlandish I would not want to do. I have come to believe God's will for me is to take care of the responsibilities in my present day life the best way I can.

MEDITATION FOR TODAY

If I pray for anything specific today, may I understand that You will hear me and respond.

TODAY I WILL REMEMBER

God always answers prayers: sometimes, yes; sometimes, no; sometimes, wait.

June 27

The fear of the pain of acute depression remains with those who have suffered in the throes of it. The agony of being so hopeless lingers in our memories. The total apathy of our lives during that time is not easy to forget. Yet it is wrong to be preoccupied with our past ailments. A look back to remember what life was like can be healthy in that it is reassuring to see how far we have come. Only those of us who have been there can know what the person now suffering from depression is going through. Only we can prove that it can and will get better. By sharing our pasts we can improve ours and others' futures.

MEDITATION FOR TODAY

May my past struggle with depression prove valuable to someone else.

TODAY I WILL REMEMBER

Don't dwell; just tell.

June 28

REFLECTION FOR TODAY

How much of my life has been spent wallowing in guilt instead of taking action? The Program teaches that this sick pleasure is one of the dubious luxuries I cannot afford. If I feel guilty today, I can use that guilt to propel me into action, admitting my fault (Steps Five and Ten), making amends (Step Nine). When I have done my best to correct what I did, I am free to forgive myself. EA is a Program of action, not retrospection. I cannot carry a heavy burden of guilt any more.

MEDITATION FOR TODAY

Let me be clear about where I was at fault, and fearless and thorough in making amends. Help me to accept the response even if it is not what I had hoped for.

TODAY I WILL REMEMBER

To travel lightly through life without the wreckage of the past.

June 29

I am a winner! What a perfect way to start the day - reminding myself that with my Higher Power's help, I can accomplish what I need to today. The old saying, "where there's a will there's a way" applies to me today. If obstacles appear, I will remember there is always a way to hurdle them. I will have the determination and strength to keep going until I reach my goals. I will not become discouraged and will have enough faith to persevere, knowing in my heart and mind that I truly am a winner.

MEDITATION FOR TODAY

Thank You, God, for the strength You give me to carry on.

TODAY I WILL REMEMBER

I am a winner in the game of life.

June 30

REFLECTION FOR TODAY

When I first came into the Program, I did not believe in God. I had decided there was no God. According to my thinking, there was too much suffering in the world and in my life for there to be a God. Life did not work the way I wanted and I was not getting my way. I concluded there could not be a God. Step Two said a power greater than myself could restore me to sanity. I had to become open to believing in a power greater than myself.

MEDITATION FOR TODAY

Help me to be willing to surrender my old ideas about You and to develop new ones.

TODAY I WILL REMEMBER

Misbelief, disbelief, and no belief produce my miseries.

July

July 1

REFLECTION FOR TODAY

When we share our problems and troubles with another understanding human being, we are doing each of us a favor. We are helping ourselves just by speaking about what is bothering us. Sometimes just the speaking of it aloud will supply the solution for us. If there is not an immediate answer, we feel better simply because we did talk about it. There is always the possibility the other person can help us. By sharing our worries, we are letting the other person know of our trust and caring for them. This makes for good feelings. We also, in a sense, are telling the other person we will be there for them under similar circumstances.

MEDITATION FOR TODAY

May You always provide me with a warm, understanding friend who will share my troubles.

TODAY I WILL REMEMBER

Talk about it!

July 2

REFLECTION FOR TODAY

Before I can love anyone else I have to accept and love myself. Healthy self-love is necessary in my daily living with and loving those around me. "Love your neighbor as yourself" does not say instead of yourself. Until I recognize the good and beautiful things in me and love me just as I am - the good, the bad, and the ugly - I cannot love another nor can I truly begin replacing the character flaws I find in myself.

MEDITATION FOR TODAY

May I begin each day with a realization of my good qualities and always be grateful for them.

TODAY I WILL REMEMBER

I will be positive and grateful for the goodness within me.

July 3

REFLECTION FOR TODAY

What is it that brings on an emotional slip? How and why does it happen? These quesions have answers which only I can supply, but it helps if I write down the persons, places, and things or events in connection with each peevish or painful state. The "touchy spots" or thoughts which seem to come before or during such times can give me a clue as to what my Higher Power would have me do. What Step am I on? When was my last meeting? My last call to reach out? When did I last read some solid program literature? In my writings or journal, have I noted those things which successfully pulled me out of a negative emotional state? What worked for me then? Sometimes a simple thing comes to mind, a tool given us in this Program such as HALT (the four elements which frequently bring on bad emotional states: hunger, anger, loneliness, and tiredness).

MEDITATION FOR TODAY

Thank You for these simple, effective tools.

TODAY I WILL REMEMBER

I will steer clear of HALT and consider what effect they have had in my life so far.

July 4

REFLECTION FOR TODAY

We have traditionally celebrated the Fourth of July (or Independence Day) in the United States with family picnics, parades, and fireworks. Fireworks is a good description of my behavior at many of these family gatherings. On past holidays my emotions erupted like skyrockets and Roman candles. Words came out of my mouth like firecrackers - loud, fast, and hurtful. Thanks to my Higher Power and EA, holidays have become a meaningful and enjoyable part of my life. I have learned to live and enjoy life even though there are unsolved problems.

MEDITATION FOR TODAY

Thank You for holidays and loved ones with whom we can enjoy them. They bring an added spice and zest to my life.

TODAY I WILL REMEMBER

An anticipated holiday is no longer fearful to me.

July 5

Love makes me vulnerable. When I love someone, I grow close to him or her. This person can see my soft spots and knows what hurts me. I have hurt so much already I do not want to hurt any more so I start to back off hoping if I keep a safe distance I will cut down my chances of getting hurt. I also limit my chances of finding intimate relationships. I could end up living in a superficial, non-committal environment where caring and sharing would only be words. Being close to someone is a risk, but it is also a delight. The person who knows what really hurts me is also the person who knows what makes me happy and how to put a sparkle in my eye, a spring in my step, and a song in my heart. The distance I keep between myself and my loved ones keeps out hurt but also keeps out joy.

MEDITATION FOR TODAY

Give me the courage to get close enough to take a chance on getting joy into my life.

TODAY I WILL REMEMBER

I can keep out hurt but I can also keep out joy.

July 6

We dream of being winners. In our fantasies we are always the successful achievers. In order for these dreams to come true, we have to *want* to be winners. With wanting something comes drive, determination, and a sense of commitment. When we take a good look at the winners we admire, we see they *look* like winners. They have a pride in their appearance. They *talk* like winners and converse with others with ease. They are comfortable with any group. They *act* like winners and it is easy to see self-esteem and self-confidence radiate from them. These same people *think* like winners and have no room in their heads for negative thoughts. Seeing the positive side has become a habit with them and eventually their way of life.

MEDITATION FOR TODAY

Help me acquire "winners' ways."

TODAY I WILL REMEMBER

My success starts with the attitude in my head; not the circumstance of my birth.

July 7

REFLECTION FOR TODAY

After I had been in the Program for awhile and was still impatient with my growth, emotionally as well as spiritually, I had to realize I had probably neglected to see the small positive changes occurring within me. At first I had to look hard to find those small positive changes which later grew into giant positive changes. Now I realize those changes were there all along. Because I was not satisfied with them, I discounted the little seeds which just needed more water and warm sunshine (EA) to grow. Those seeds were permanently planted no matter what I believed. And yet, I still became frustrated because I was tired of my shortcomings and wanted a miracle, which was to become well right then and there. I had no patience with my very slow progress.

MEDITATION FOR TODAY

May I have trust and faith that I will be better if I take action and search for what I need.

TODAY I WILL REMEMBER

I can feel better about myself just knowing I am at least trying to improve.

July 8

REFLECTION FOR TODAY

Recognition is a basic human need. Recognition can come from conditional strokes which are given for performance. Conditional strokes separate the behavior from the person and they are earned. Recognition can also come from unconditional strokes which are generally given non-verbally by a look or a touch. Unconditional strokes are just for being and they are unearnable. We need relationships where we are given unconditional strokes for without them we cannot develop a healthy self-esteem. Interestingly, no amount of conditional strokes we can rally by doing things to please others will ever compensate for our need to experience the value that only unconditional strokes provide.

MEDITATION FOR TODAY

Help me to be open to the positive characteristics in others. Encourage me to affirm their positive qualities.

TODAY I WILL REMEMBER

The more I value myself, the better equipped I will be to give others unconditional strokes.

July 9

REFLECTION FOR TODAY

Each day brings new challenges to meet and I am given the choice as to how I will meet those challenges. I can feel defeated, give up, feel sorry for myself and not try or I can optimistically give my best to the situation, think about the positive aspects, and enthusiastically await the results of my efforts. If the results are those desired, the credit should go to my Higher Power. If the results are of a disastrous nature, I have no need to feel defeated and unhappy because if I have allowed my Higher Power to be a part of my daily life, that Higher Power can assume the responsibility for the failure.

MEDITATION FOR TODAY

Be my guide as I assess my successes and attitudes. Give me the courage to go beyond what I have already done.

TODAY I WILL REMEMBER

Sitting in a chair doing nothing will not make my life exciting and productive.

July 10

REFLECTION FOR TODAY

Emotional pain is what brought me to EA. In spite of my fear, I went to my first meeting and found I was not alone. I also found hope. I heard how others had found help through the Twelve Steps and through sharing with each other, and I made the commitment to give it a try. I attended weekly meetings, read the literature, and tried to work the Program in my daily life. After spurts of growth and slips, I realized I was getting better. The anxiety, panic, and abnormal fears were beginning to lessen. I continue to attend meetings to maintain what I have learned and to continue to grow as a person through my faith in my Higher Power. When I give hope to a new member by telling my recovery story, my growth is enhanced.

MEDITATION FOR TODAY

God, help me to remember the past pain. Help me to be grateful to the Program and the people who have shared their thoughts, feelings, fears, and faith with me. Let me never forget to look to You for guidance and to know You will support me.

TODAY I WILL REMEMBER

Through pain comes growth and eventually peace and serenity.

July 11

REFLECTION FOR TODAY

I spent a good share of my life feeling inferior to others. Because of this feeling, I continually compared myself with them. I compared my weaknesses with their strengths and, of course, I fell short. Once I learned that comparing myself was a copout for not developing my own creativity and talents, it became easier to let go of this defense. Becoming willing to let go of my comparing has opened me to creativity and talent I never dreamed I had.

MEDITATION FOR TODAY

If I begin to compare myself to someone else, give me a little push.

TODAY I WILL REMEMBER

I have a great deal to offer by just being me.

July 12

REFLECTION FOR TODAY

Growth is a continual process. There is always something new we can learn. Each time we are willing to risk, we are once again led along the path to a new encounter. As we accept the challenge which the new path brings us to, we often discover abilities we did not know we possessed. Gratitude for our new abilities will expand our freedom and fill us with much joy.

MEDITATION FOR TODAY

May I never forget to be thankful for my new life.

TODAY I WILL REMEMBER

I will be open, I will take a risk, and I will take time to say thanks.

July 13

REFLECTION FOR TODAY

I had fears of what God would ask me to be and do; fears of a life I did not want to lead. Slowly my faith has developed to where I am willing and able to turn my life over to God. Piece by piece I have ventured to give up control of my will and life and let God have control. Many times I take control back. At no time has it worked out better for me to have been in control rather than God. Every time God has been in control, it has worked out for the best. My spiritual progress has been gradual. As my trust in God has grown, the areas I surrender to my Higher Power have increased.

MEDITATION FOR TODAY

May I commit myself to letting You handle my life today.

TODAY I WILL REMEMBER

In God's control, I am in the best care possible.

July 14

REFLECTION FOR TODAY

Pride and fear have been my worst enemies. Pride says, "You do not have to look," and fear says, "You dare not look." To grow, both pride and fear have to be put on the shelf. Each time I face these enemies, I break through another barrier. Breaking through the barriers brings me more in touch with the caring and loving person I was created to be; plus, I gain a sense of belonging I had always wanted but did not know how to achieve.

MEDITATION FOR TODAY

May I have the ability to be honest with myself to avoid needless pain.

TODAY I WILL REMEMBER

If I feel pride or fear, I will reach out in spite of it.

July 15

REFLECTION FOR TODAY

Let me remember how the dawn breaks in the morning. The change from darkness into light comes on so gradually it is hardly noticeable. But at one point I become able to discern forms where before has been complete darkness. And everything around me becomes clearer almost imperceptibly up to the moment when the sun rises in all its splendor, flooding the glorious beauty of the earth with its golden, warming rays. Let me think about this whenever I am feeling impatient.

MEDITATION FOR TODAY

May I put my whole reliance in You, trusting that You (who lets the sun rise over us every day) are taking care of all Your children.

TODAY I WILL REMEMBER

Dawn comes slowly and so will my patience.

July 16

REFLECTION FOR TODAY

My fears came from lack of self-confidence which usually meant lack of confidence in God. I used up so much energy worrying about what might happen that I had no energy left to handle the situation when or if it arose. Someone suggested that I asked myself, "What is the worst thing that could happen?" and to imagine myself walking through that scene. Instead of asking *"what* if", act *"as* if" I had the confidence to handle the situation. Feeling and acting more confident was often enough to carry me through.

MEDITATION FOR TODAY

May I remember that my self-confidence comes from confidence in You.

TODAY I WILL REMEMBER

Nothing can happen today that God and I cannot handle together.

July 17

My written inventory must be thorough, going back to my earliest memories because this is where the root of my problem is. It was in childhood I developed a pattern of behavior which I thought would protect me from hurt, assure me of financial and emotional security, and gain approval and praise for myself. Step Four is an ego-reducer. To get to this Step I have had to admit I have not been able to gain peace of mind and emotional stability by applying my old patterns of behavior and thinking.

MEDITATION FOR TODAY

May I realize that You will accept my sincere attempt to search out my strengths as well as my weaknesses.

TODAY I WILL REMEMBER

I do not have to do things perfectly for God's approval.

July 18

REFLECTION FOR TODAY

There was a time when I had innumerable dreadful anxiety attacks. They left me fearful of many things and full of panic. There were times when I could not leave my home because of them. For the most part, they have gone away since I started working the Program. Occasionally one will appear for no apparent reason (even when I am working the Program to the utmost) and, for a moment, the panic comes again. I also get angry because I feel I no longer *should* have these attacks. If I stop then and there and say to myself, "I accept that I am having an anxiety attack and I surrender it to my Higher Power", it will usually go away - not instantaneously, but soon.

MEDITATION FOR TODAY

May I always remember that acceptance and surrender are effective tools for handling anxiety attacks.

TODAY I WILL REMEMBER

Don't panic! Accept.

July 19

REFLECTION FOR TODAY

The healing which continues to come as a result of working this Program is astounding. There is so much more to gain than just ridding ourselves of our addictions and compulsions. As I am willing to be open and honest and reach out for support, and as I am willing to go through some very painful times, my sense of freedom and aliveness continues to expand. This freedom and aliveness are wonderful gifts - gifts for which I am very grateful.

MEDITATION FOR TODAY

May I not be willing to settle for only ridding myself of my addictions and compulsions. May I have the courage to continue expanding and becoming all You have created me to be.

TODAY I WILL REMEMBER

The painful times are worthwhile when I can look back and see how much love I have been able to let into my life.

July 20

REFLECTION FOR TODAY

Sometimes I work too hard, get too busy, and run rough-shod over problems - my own and maybe others. I often ignore this too busy problem for a while. After all, these many, many things I have to get done are very, very important! But wait a minute. They are not nearly as important as taking care of myself, getting the necessary sleep, eating properly, and taking some time to communicate in a loving way with persons in my family and in my life in general. But the tough thing is to make choices; often because I have to choose between several things I want to do, or things that other people want me to do. Making choices is not easy. I need to ask myself if what I am so busy at is really as important as some of the other things which are calling for some time.

MEDITATION FOR TODAY

May I slow down at least enough to take a quick inventory now and then. Help me to put myself on the list.

TODAY I WILL REMEMBER

To realize the most important thing is to be *alive* in the world.

July 21

I am responsible *to* others; but I am responsible *for* only myself. When I take responsibility for another's happiness, I set myself up for defeat. Poor me - I try so hard! Self-pity envelopes me. I pout for a while but I struggle back to my feet and meddle in their lives again. Only when I see that I am overly involved in my family's lives, smothering them and hindering their growth, can I have a more mature understanding of responsibility. The hard part for me is taking charge of my own life. I see how I have avoided that responsibility by leaning too heavily on others for my sense of self-worth.

MEDITATION FOR TODAY

Remind me that my self-worth is my responsibility.

TODAY I WILL REMEMBER

To mind my own business.

July 22

REFLECTION FOR TODAY

In the past I have tied my self-worth to how well I have done the things I have strived to do. When I didn't do well, I felt worthless. When I first came into the Program, I fell into the same trap. Through the Program I have come to realize that my value as a person is independent of how well I do any given thing, including working my Program. I am not a better, more worthwhile person when I am working my Program well. I am, however, able to enjoy a richer, more fulfilling, and more serene life when I do.

MEDITATION FOR TODAY

May I realize I will not be a more worthwhile person if I live my Program well today - only a happier one.

TODAY I WILL REMEMBER

I can work toward serenity knowing I am already a valuable person.

July 23

REFLECTION FOR TODAY

Today I took my two-year old son to the carnival where he rode on a tiny fire truck with no less than nine steering wheels, none of which could actually turn the vehicle. My son was nevertheless very serious and spun the wheel furiously as did the other children beside him. Isn't this how God must see us as "children" many times · intent on what actually means so little and controlling so little of where we really are going?

MEDITATION FOR TODAY

When I find life grim or think the stakes are high, let me recall again that I am in a spiritual childhood, and you wish me to enjoy my ride through life.

TODAY I WILL REMEMBER

I need not take myself so seriously!

July 24

Over and over in the Program I have heard that anger and resentment are our number one enemies. This does not mean I am to deny the anger or resentment I may feel at times. What it does mean is that I need to deal with these emotions in the present so they do not again gain power over me and my behavior. Feelings I deny will always find an outlet. The more open and honest I can be, the less power anger and resentment will have in my life again.

MEDITATION FOR TODAY

Because I am so uncomfortable with my anger, help me to be honest when it is present or else it will build up and snowball into self-defeating behavior.

TODAY I WILL REMEMBER

Being human, I will continue to experience the gamut of emotions including anger and resentment.

July 25

REFLECTION FOR TODAY

For some reason it was harder for me to forgive myself than it was to forgive others. I was always stricter with myself. I expected more and better from me. It was easier to justify other peoples' apparent mistakes. In my mind it was okay for others to be human, but not me. I seemed to have such high expectations for myself and felt I must be the best and do the best always. It was so easy to criticize myself and my actions. I have learned and now practice self-forgiveness. I cannot forgive others properly if I cannot forgive me. When I forgive myself I find the courage to begin again. I now know I do not have to be perfect. What a relief!

MEDITATION FOR TODAY

Remind me always that if You can forgive me, I can forgive me.

TODAY I WILL REMEMBER

Forgiveness is love.

July 26

REFLECTION FOR TODAY

We live, grow, and are better people because of our Program. How could anyone reject it? I was ready for the Program three weeks after I heard about it. Another person may have been sitting in meetings for six months and still not be in the groove. Why? People learn and live at their own pace. I cannot manipulate or push someone into my schedule of growth. While some grow by leaps and bounds, others grow inch by inch. Progress is what we strive for. Speed is not a top priority.

MEDITATION FOR TODAY

Give me the patience and tolerance to understand someone else's (as well as my own) pace of growth.

TODAY I WILL REMEMBER

We did not get sick overnight nor will we get well overnight, but we will get well.

July 27

REFLECTION FOR TODAY

Today is my spouse's birthday. The best gift I can give him is to let him be himself — not try to change him. He has the same rights as I do and is entitled to make his own decisions whether I think they are correct or not. Criticism is a major character defect of mine - one that I ask my Higher Power to remove. It is a very unloving habit and only leads to arguments and bad feelings.

MEDITATION FOR TODAY

Help me to remember I cannot change anybody but myself.

TODAY I WILL REMEMBER

I will concentrate today on *my own* assets and character defects and I will be grateful for those who love me as I am.

July 28

REFLECTION FOR TODAY

Whenever I "perform", I split myself into two halves; the performer and the observer/critic. Trying to perform allows that ever present screamer sitting on my shoulder the chance to unleash a dose of self-hate from the reservoir I have built and maintained during my life. The chance may be the most minor mistake or insignificant admission on my part. This can happen in any circumstance - from building a coffee table to talking at a meeting. On the other hand, when I "participate", I minimize self-consciousness and the chance of embarrassment. When I am participating, I am sharing the real me; and being the real me destroys any need for that internal critic. I realize that my failures are more valuable to my emotional growth than any of my successes. My past life has too often shown that my successes temporarily blinded me to the reality of my human limitations. I need to use these limitations as checks and balances in my struggle to know God's will for me.

MEDITATION FOR TODAY

God, continue to grant me one of Your most wonderful gifts - the right to be human.

TODAY I WILL REMEMBER

Participating keeps me whole(some).

July 29

REFLECTION FOR TODAY

"Acceptance" - the magic word in my life. It is through acceptance that I have found all the treasures which I have searched for all my life....love, foregiveness, serenity, caring, sharing and compassion. These marvels have come into my life because of my acceptance of: myself - just the way I am today; others - just the way they are today; things I cannot change and those I can. The acceptance of a Higher Power in my life has made me realize that it is only through that Higher Power that all these gifts have come to me.

MEDITATION FOR TODAY

Remind me that it is only through acceptance I will find the answers I need to live a life full of freedom and joy.

TODAY I WILL REMEMBER

People, places, and things are fine just the way they are.

July 30

REFLECTION FOR TODAY

I have learned to watch what I say because the words I use, both in my mind and orally, can affect me and others. If I use pessimistic, sad, or angry words, I tend to feel and behave in that way. When I use optimistic, happy, and loving words, I react in those ways. When I speak constructive and joyful words, people around me seem to be happier and to respond in the same positive manner. My words can be powerful and influence me and others. I must select them with care. It helps if I stop to think before I speak.

MEDITATION FOR TODAY

Please inspire my words today and let them be an expression of good.

TODAY I WILL REMEMBER

I will use my eye teeth to watch my words.

July 31

REFLECTION FOR TODAY

If I owed a debt and paid it in full, would I continue to pay that same debt? If I did, my sanity would be questioned. Yet I returned to my Higher Power again and again asking forgiveness for the same thing. By hanging on to my guilt, I was unable to be receptive to growth and healing. I no longer believe I have to condemn myself, even for not living up to my own reasonable expectations. Once I have made amends, I need to be willing to forgive myself.

MEDITATION FOR TODAY

If I begin to hang on to guilt, remind me how defeating this behavior is.

TODAY I WILL REMEMBER

To hang on to guilt is to cop out.

August

August 1

When I turn my eyes inward and dwell on my fear, the fear seems to grow. The longer I look at it, the larger it looms until it obsesses my life and I am scared stiff. Once I accepted the forgiveness of my Higher Power for my past "failures", I began to accept myself and my humanness. My eyeballs look outward. One of the strange things I have noticed is that all the things I was afraid might happen, did not. The rent and the bills got paid and life went on. Because of the serenity which has slowly seeped into my life, I am able to cope with the problems that confront me. I have a clear mind and a quieted soul.

MEDITATION FOR TODAY

Keep my eyes facing out toward the day at hand and upward to You for strength.

TODAY I WILL REMEMBER

No more ingrown eyeballs.

August 2

REFLECTION FOR TODAY

Too many occasions flit by without my recognizing the kindnesses and good done for me. It seems as if my life consists of mundane, repetitive routines of the day before. Nothing spectacular seems to be happening, nothing for which to be thankful. Yet my yesterday was a miracle. I was able to take care of my responsibilities with no complications, Everything happened as it should. That, in itself, would elicit thankfulness on the part of those who have physical disabilities or other adversities to overcome, but I take it for granted and credit myself with the power to control my own life and the ability to succeed where I so desire. That is not true because my Higher Power is the source of my success. My Higher Power uses ordinary people to help in making my life as smooth and problem free as it usually is.

MEDITATION FOR TODAY

Help me to be more appreciative and grateful for the life which has been given to me.

TODAY I WILL REMEMBER

To give thanks for each and every thing.

August 3

Grief can be devastating and debilitating. It can continue to creep into our lives years after the experience which caused it. It can and does appear at the most unexpected and unwanted times. Part of grief is anger and guilt which seems unacceptable to most of us. Whether the pain comes from the loss of a spouse, significant other, pet, job, boss, child, limb, or house does not matter. The pain is just as strong and seemingly unendurable. Words do not help at these times. We need courage to just breathe and exist. If we can focus on living a moment at a time, strength will eventually come. We cannot let grief prevent us from loving again. It is a part of living which we all must go through.

MEDITATION FOR TODAY

Help me to remember that You and time are my best friends in my struggle with grief.

TODAY I WILL REMEMBER

It is good to mourn but there comes a time to get beyond the sorrow and resume a happier life.

August 4

There is little that can bring more happiness or heartache than sex. Sex is an essential part of my being which I am continually learning about. At times I have approached it by rushing in irresponsibly. At times I have tried to run away from it. Today I am learning a better balance. The Twelve Steps are teaching me to be diligently honest and this seems to be the key to sexual harmony. I am learning to ask if the needs of my partner are as important as my own. I am finding there are periods where celibacy is actually a positive step in my growth. As I place my sex life in the hands of my Higher Power, I come to know a growing contentment.

MEDITATION FOR TODAY

Guide me, Friend of my Highest Understanding, to keep sex beautiful.

TODAY I WILL REMEMBER

I will express my sexuality with love.

August 5

REFLECTION FOR TODAY

Each day consists of twenty-four hours. Perhaps I have made commitments which require some part of that time each day. I must also realize that taking care of my physical, spiritual, and mental needs requires some of that time. One of the greatest gifts I give myself is my daily time of meditation. In these quiet, still moments apart from the mainstream of my life I am able to view people and events from a different perspective. I am open to my inner voice and to the guidance of my Higher Power. My spirit is refreshed and strengthened through this as surely as my body is nourished by food and drink.

MEDITATION FOR TODAY

Thank You for being the counselor of my innermost self.

TODAY I WILL REMEMBER

I am responsible for my life, including how to spend my time.

August 6

REFLECTION FOR TODAY

One easy word of approval has the ability to change even the most bizarre state of affairs. One easy word of gratitude spoken with honesty has the ability to ease the worst possible situation. I sometimes have difficulty speaking words of approval and gratitude when in the midst of heated controversy. I have seen, however, the power brought about by praise and appreciation. I practice using these words and though they may seem awkward to my lips at first, they soon become more natural. Who can resist a compliment? Who does not appreciate gratitude? It is rewarding for me to show approval and gratitude each day to the people who share my life and make it rich and complete. I must not neglect myself when I praise and appreciate.

MEDITATION FOR TODAY

May I show my appreciation and gratitude for all the blessings which will come my way this day.

TODAY I WILL REMEMBER

Thank God, other people, and me.

August 7

REFLECTION FOR TODAY

I couldn't understand why with all my faith I still didn't have peace. Then I realized I gave my troubles to my Higher Power by sending them up on a kite string and hanging on to the other end. In other words, I didn't really surrender. When I trusted another human being, it gave me strength to trust my Higher Power. This allowed me to really surrender and release the kite string which held my problems.

MEDITATION FOR TODAY

Help me to extend my gratitude to the human beings who gave me trust.

TODAY I WILL REMEMBER

God cannot help me unless I let go.

August 8

The longer I am in this Program the more aware I become of my need for basic Step One. To use this Step I have to admit my powerlessness over my emotions and admit to that surrender. How often am I still denying, fighting, or feeling guilty about my thoughts and feelings? I cannot predict, control, or even understand my thoughts and feelings fully. They are a part of my humanness - and an acceptable part of me. Only by admitting and accepting my emotions as they are can I be freed of their hold upon me.

MEDITATION FOR TODAY
Help me to stop judging myself.

TODAY I WILL REMEMBER
I will admit and accept my powerlessness.

August 9

REFLECTION FOR TODAY

Many times I put off taking action I either needed to take or wanted to take because I was afraid. This behavior only made me more fearful. Taking responsible action can change my feelings toward myself and my surroundings. It is freeing to know I do not have to stay locked into my fears. The experiences I fear, I need to face. As I face my fears, I grow in confidence and trust both my Higher Power and myself.

MEDITATION FOR TODAY

Help me to be aware today if I am putting off taking responsible action because I am afraid.

TODAY I WILL REMEMBER

Putting off taking responsible action can lead me back into my symptoms.

August 10

The words "I am not alone" have come to mean several things to me. I joined EA in search of personal recovery - a desire to become well emotionally, as did all of us. But I have learned that my recovery is aided by your recovery. As I grow, I pass it on to you and as you grow, you pass it on to others. Even though ours is, in a sense, a selfish program, I must remember that what I do for me, I do for you and vice versa. What is good for me is good for you. We are all in this together.

MEDITATION FOR TODAY

May I never forget that when I help, I am helped; what I give away is doubly returned.

TODAY I WILL REMEMBER

I am never alone.

August 11

REFLECTION FOR TODAY

The Program teaches me to take care of myself. In the old days I was self-destructive. Now I care for my own well being and nurture myself. If I am tired, I take time to rest or sleep. If I am lonely, I call a friend. I say no to people pleasing. If someone wants me to do something I know would be harmful to me, I do not do it. I do not expect others to read my mind. When I need care, I take the responsibility for myself.

MEDITATION FOR TODAY

If I slip back into my old ways, help me to remember I can be responsible for myself with Your help.

TODAY I WILL REMEMBER

No one can care for me like I can care for myself.

August 12

REFLECTION FOR TODAY

The road to self-acceptance is long and often full of pain. When we feel rejected or misunderstood, it hurts and often tempts us to question the value of our needs and feeling. The Twelve Step Program gives us the tools we need to know and accept ourselves. Although self-acceptance cannot be obtained quickly or easily, once we give ourselves completely to this simple Program, we start on the path toward valuing ourselves. All lasting happiness is dependent on a healthy love and acceptance of myself.

MEDITATION FOR TODAY

Let me not be detoured or discouraged by the pain involved in growing.

TODAY I WILL REMEMBER

I cannot be right for anyone unless I am right for myself.

August 13

REFLECTION FOR TODAY

It has been said, "That as a man thinketh in his heart, so he is." This is why a hostile man lives in a hostile world and a loving man lives in a loving world. It is the same world - it is how I perceive it that counts. I have a choice and herein lies my accountability. It has also been said, "As a man sows, so shall he reap." I must realize that thinking, feeling, or acting negatively begets negative results. What I put out, I shall receive. The effects of my words and acts have profound impact in my world, and on others as well as myself.

MEDITATION FOR TODAY

May You work through me to radiate calmness, trust, generosity, truth, justice forgiveness, acceptance, and love.

TODAY I WILL REMEMBER

Happiness and good come to me in its highest form, not because I seek to absorb it, but rather, because I seek to radiate it.

August 14

My best attempts at solving a problem may not be good enough. There are some problems in life I cannot solve and was not meant to solve, no matter how I feel about them. My job lies in recognizing which problems are truly mine, and then giving a good try at solving them with my Higher Power's help. Letting go and letting God take my problems when I have done my best is the only way to go. I am not responsible for the outcome.

MEDITATION FOR TODAY

May I realize the longer I continue to hold onto my problems and hurts, the more I blame myself or others.

TODAY I WILL REMEMBER

If I cling to my problems, I am not trusting my Higher Power.

August 15

REFLECTION FOR TODAY

There is an old saying that "laughter is the best medicine." In our emotional illness, we know how healing laughter can be. Both tears and laughter are very powerful emotional releases and perhaps it is no accident they frequently occur together. While humor can sometimes be misused as a weapon, gentle, loving laughter can be a shield against adversity. Laughter can often restore a sense of balance and perspective to our volatile, confused emotions. Laughter can cut through otherwise impenetrable barriers in our personal relationships. Laughter can reaffirm even the faintest glimmer of optimism in a failing spirit. Learning to laugh at everyday situations around us helps us to cope. Learning to laugh at the weaknesses in ourselves helps us to grow.

MEDITATION FOR TODAY

May I realize the key to learning to laugh at all is in learning to be *vulnerable* - in recognizing and accepting my powerlessness.

TODAY I WILL REMEMBER

I will share the humor I encounter today by telling God the joke I found and listening in my soul for the laughter.

August 16

As on the highways, there are directional signs in my life which warn me of possible mishaps; signs such as, HALT, which reminds me never to get too hungry, angry, lonely, or tired. My behavior can be and often is affected by any of those four feelings. If I am careful of my habits and try to be reasonable and balanced with my life, I can avoid much pain. My body tells me when it is tired or hungry. I must watch for my body's red light which says, "STOP". It is time to rest or eat. My mind tells me when I am angry and lonely. I must watch for my mind's amber light which says, "SLOW DOWN". Paying attention to my own signals is as important as following highway signs.

MEDITATION FOR TODAY
Help me to see ALL of the signs in my life.

TODAY I WILL REMEMBER
I will watch for my red, amber, and green lights.

August 17

REFLECTION FOR TODAY

Most of us expended a great deal of energy trying to be perfect. Of course we failed. The more we tried to be perfect, the more aware we became of our weaknesses and our faults. Interestingly enough, we were created both human and divine. We have the capacity of acting both as angel or beast. The more we are able to accept our weaknesses, as well as our strengths, the more peaceful we will become. The Program continues to give us a direction in gaining a greater and greater level of self-acceptance.

MEDITATION FOR TODAY

May I never lose track of the fact that I am both angel and beast.

TODAY I WILL REMEMBER

When I fall short, I will not judge myself. I will accept myself as the human being I was meant to be.

August 18

REFLECTION FOR TODAY

When a person really wants something, that person is likely to go to any lengths to gain it, even through negative behavior. Many times we do things we later regret then wonder why we responded in the way we did. As we learn about ourselves and our behavior, we see how rationalizing our actions had become a way of life and how often we were drawn toward experiences which could hurt us. This can be called the enormity of our illness. Left to ourselves, we often continue to act out defeating behavior. With the help of the Program, a Higher Power, and others, we realize we do not have to be controlled by our impulses.

MEDITATION FOR TODAY

May I stop, reach out for support, and trust a friend can help me discontinue hurting myself.

TODAY I WILL REMEMBER

I deserve to be happy and productive.

August 19

REFLECTION FOR TODAY

The intrinsic value of love is hard to measure or describe. Love encourages brotherhood and acceptance of others. It allows appreciation of one's surroundings. Love is easily detected in how one responds to annoyances and diversity. It promotes thinking of the positive aspects of daily situations rather than on the negative failures and shortcomings. Love is being truthful in our relationships with others and is expressed in our response to everyday life because it is not limited by boundaries.

MEDITATION FOR TODAY

Help me to sincerely love and appreciate the life I am privileged to live each day.

TODAY I WILL REMEMBER

Love without truth is not good; neither is truth without love.

August 20

REFLECTION FOR TODAY

"Are you angry and upset about what happened?" "Who, me? Heavens no. I do not let things like that bother me." Sound familiar? It is the first denial of a feeling - saving face and trying to preserve my "I don't care" attitude. Now I start to think and mull the incident over in my mind. It consumes me. My stomach starts to churn as resentment begins to build. "No, nothing is bothering me. I'm just tired." Second denial. My concentration is shot and I cannot think. Disorientation has my mind whirling. A sudden noise or question from a child or a broken dish starts up my yelling machine. "No, NOTHING IS WRONG! LEAVE ME ALONE!" Third denial. Hopefully the yelling has allowed me to let off some steam. If not, the next phase could be striking out physically at the persons closest to me. Now let me turn the clock back to the beginning. "Are you angry and upset?" "Yes, I am. Let's talk this out and get it settled right now." No denial, no turmoil, no temporary pain. What a difference!

MEDITATION FOR TODAY

Give me the courage to admit and accept my feelings instead of denying them.

TODAY I WILL REMEMBER

Nipping it in the bud can save me from full blossomed pain.

August 21

REFLECTION FOR TODAY

A garden does not grow in one day. As I learn to live the EA Program, I will try to tend to the daily task of nurturing my own mental, physical, and spiritual growth. The exercise of a daily program will help my growth in two ways: regular practice will strengthen my self-discipline while consistent attention to my needs will foster positive growth just as scheduled watering, fertilizing, and pruning encourage healthy growth in a garden.

MEDITATION FOR TODAY

Guide my steps toward my own mental, physical, and spiritual health.

TODAY I WILL REMEMBER

Small steps repeated over and over in the course of time become a great journey.

August 22

Negativism can lead me astray faster than anything else I know of. It is so easy for me to catch this virus of negativity. The germs surround me. If people around me are in a pessimistic mood, it is contagious to me. Then the negativity leads to depression which in turn leads to self-pity and all the other diseases which follow. When I hear myself say, "I can't," "I shouldn't," or "It's a rotten day," I have to alert myself to the possibility of a major epidemic of symptoms and pain. I must remove myself from the negative atmosphere. I must speak with someone who is positive and I must think positive thoughts. With concentration and effort I can cure the virus.

MEDITATION FOR TODAY

Position me on the positive path and push me in that direction.

TODAY I WILL REMEMBER

Negativity makes me ill; positivity keeps me healthy.

August 23

REFLECTION FOR TODAY

If I have talents and abilities in a certain area where someone else does not, does it make me any more special in my Creator's eyes? I do not believe it does. There was a time when I thought people were better because of the things they could do. Now I believe if someone has been given a particular talent, it is his or her responsibility to develop it. Talents do not make someone better - only different.

MEDITATION FOR TODAY

Grant me the courage to stop comparing and to begin looking at my own talents for they are there.

TODAY I WILL REMEMBER

God has given each of us talents and abilities which will fulfill us if only we have the courage to follow our intuition.

August 24

REFLECTION FOR TODAY

The Program teaches that fear may come from projecting what might happen. That is not living one day at a time. One way I learned to deal with fear is to organize. I make a list of six things which I have to do. I learn to recognize the time of day when my mind is freshest and I have the most energy. I do the most difficult or most urgent thing at that time (First Things First) and I concentrate on that item and do not think of anything else. The feeling of accomplishment I get gives me the momentum to do the next thing on the list. That list becomes less frightening.

MEDITATION FOR TODAY

May I remember that God gives me the strength to do what needs to be done if I ask.

TODAY I WILL REMEMBER

One day at a time may mean one item on the list at a time.

August 25

REFLECTION FOR TODAY

Learning to overcome fear with faith is a lot like learning to swim. Reading about swimming is of little help; neither is watching other swimmers. Sooner or later we must trust the water to hold us up. To do this we must risk jumping into the water. So it is with faith - it *will* buoy us up. But first we must enter an unfamiliar medium; then we must practice.

MEDITATION FOR TODAY

May I trust the principles and fellowship of EA to sustain me as I practice to overcome the fear in my life. Ours is the way of faith; not fear.

TODAY I WILL REMEMBER

In our fellowship I am afloat on a sea of love.

August 26

REFLECTION FOR TODAY

I am not God. I cannot control others I love. I do not own their problems; therefore, I must learn to leave them in God's care. After all, God loves them even more than I do and wants only good things for them. The Higher Power's plans for them are far superior to anything that my manipulating and scheming could bring about. What a relief not to be God!

MEDITATION FOR TODAY

May I be grateful that You are there to guide and protect my loved ones.

TODAY I WILL REMEMBER

God can and will do it!

August 27

So often I either denied my feelings or was not aware of them. I tried to avoid feelings because I did not want to feel pain. It was imperative that I came to see pain from a new perspective. Pain does not come from God. Feeling pain is part of my being human. Pain tells me I need to change something (maybe only my attitude). If a person did not feel pain from a physical illness, a doctor might not be seen, which could result in death. Pain is necessary.

MEDITATION FOR TODAY

If I am trying to avoid pain again, help me to remember that pain is not all negative. The fact is: there is no gain without pain.

TODAY I WILL REMEMBER

Pain is inevitable - suffering is optional.

August 28

REFLECTION FOR TODAY

In the Fourth Step we write down not only our character defects, but we also list our positive traits. Why can't I realize the power I have to improve my emotional health by using these gifts - these traits which make me feel good about myself and make those around me feel good too? My sense of humor is number one on my list of positive qualities. The best person to use it for is *me*. Laughing at myself helps me to be humble and to accept myself even when I goof. When others are down and I can make them laugh, we both benefit.

MEDITATION FOR TODAY

Help me to develop a sense of humor and appreciate laughter in my life.

TODAY I WILL REMEMBER

I believe God is a healer and that laughter is one of God's prescriptions.

August 29

Emotional honesty is one of the hardest things to acquire. It takes work and conscious effort, in the midst of anger, to ask myself why I am angry. It is easier to blame others for my feelings. Healing comes from acknowledging the feelings are mine and I have a choice. This is emotional honesty. I can never have serenity if I let others upset me. I can fight my feelings or say they are the fault of others. If I accept that this is the way I feel, I can keep going and know that, "This too shall pass" even if I don't have a solution to the problem. I can choose a course of action to correct the situation.

MEDITATION FOR TODAY
I pray for the wisdom to know the difference.

TODAY I WILL REMEMBER
Being honest with myself brings peace.

August 30

I never understood why my life was so unre-
warding, or what it meant to "let go" until EA
taught me that the opposite of "Let Go and Let
God" is like driving through life with the
emergency brake on. Everything is harder except for complete stops which correspond to my
periods of total withdrawal. After driving a
while though, friction builds up inside and my
brakes smoke angrily. I push harder and harder
on the gas yet less and less gets done. Finally the
brakes may wear out altogether and I go wildly
out of control causing chaos all around me.

MEDITATION FOR TODAY

Without the security which You give me, my
control on life causes me to wear out premature-
ly. May I loosen up and give my life to You
today.

TODAY I WILL REMEMBER

To release the emergency brake and trust that
God will tell me when I need to slow down.

August 31

REFLECTION FOR TODAY

One of the most difficult growth periods we are apt to experience is the loss of a friend. This person is not able to go along with us on our journey of self-discovery and healing. The loss can cause a great deal of pain and sadness. Yet if we remain open, we will be aware that our Higher Power has put a new relationship in our path, someone who can give us the care and nurturing we need to continue growing. We need friends to support and nurture us, particularly through difficult times. Without a caring friend we may not be able to learn about a part of ourselves we need to discover.

MEDITATION FOR TODAY

May I be the kind of friend I would like others to be for me.

TODAY I WILL REMEMBER

To have a friend I need to be a friend. I will be accepting and non-judgemental of my friends.

September

September 1

I grew up with the idea that God was sitting with a great ledger and a pen poised next to my name. Every time I made another mistake, a black mark appeared by my name because I had been so "bad". I realize now that in much of what I did I was using others' values as a criteria for what I should be. It is possible to see now that whatever I did that was "bad" was not unique. It had been done before. None of us are clever enough to come up with "something new". Have I stopped using the standards of the world to govern my behavior?

MEDITATION FOR TODAY

God, I know that You will do for me what I cannot do for myself. Help me remember You will accept me with all of my imperfections.

TODAY I WILL REMEMBER

My imperfections are a sign of my humanness.

September 2

REFLECTION FOR TODAY

Through recognizing and admitting my powerlessness, I am able to acknowledge my need for a Higher Power. As I acknowledge this need, I am better able to seek and accept the help of a Higher Power. I do not like to see my own weaknesses. It makes me aware that I am not, nor will I ever be, in control of my own life. This is a scary thought but at the same time, it is comforting. It takes away the responsibility of having all the answers. I do not have them nor do I have to. I need to live one day at a time trusting my Higher Power for assistance.

MEDITATION FOR TODAY

May I let go and let You.

TODAY I WILL REMEMBER

Today I will find strength in my weakness.

September 3

REFLECTION FOR TODAY

We often take on the problems of the world. We let our feelings of despair overpower us. Life provides many reasons for concern, fear, and depression. Do I want to give up and stay sick by allowing people and situations to instill me with fear, anger, defeat, and hopelessness? At times watching the news can affect me negatively. I do not have to give in to this. I can choose who and what I listen to. Above all I can choose what I let affect me. I can choose my life style. I can let go of the negative elements after deciding how I want to react to them.

MEDITATION FOR TODAY

Help me to remember I am often powerless over my circumstances — what I hear, who I am with, etc. Knowing this, with Your help, I can choose how much effect these things and people have on me.

TODAY I WILL REMEMBER

To "run with the winners" when possible. When not possible, "don't let the turkeys get me down."

September 4

Talking to my Higher Power can be like chatting with an old friend on a long distance call only it doesn't cost any money. The results are the same: a warm feeling of having spoken to someone I love and who loves me. I feel wanted, appreciated, and listened to. My ideas are not ridiculed, my feelings are not laughed at, and I feel cherished. I gain approval and respect and I know once more I am okay and all is right with my world. Just a few minutes spent communicating with my Higher Power can fill my life with joy. Why do I wait so long to take advantage of this wonder waiting for me?

MEDITATION FOR TODAY

Please dial my number when I wait too long to speak with You.

TODAY I WILL REMEMBER

I don't get a wrong number when I call God.

September 5

When I cry I am expressing my anger, fear, grief, sadness, or even happiness. I am expressing parts of me which have been so long neglected. I am glad God gave me this ability to feel my feelings. Now I wonder why I was afraid to cry. I only wish that when I was younger I could have shed tears. Now I know it is good to cry and I feel relieved. It is okay to share these feelings too.

MEDITATION FOR TODAY

Thank You, God, for I can cry and I am grateful.

TODAY I WILL REMEMBER

I can love the sadness as well as the joy.

September 6

REFLECTION FOR TODAY

So often I have read expressions like, "No one can hurt me unless I let them," or, "When you resent someone you become their slave," or that, "Anger is deadly for dependent people" in Twelve Step literature. When I heard those expressions I interpreted them to mean that if I felt these feelings, I was not working my Program. I used what I had heard to simply shut down my feelings. I have come to see that any feelings I bury will come out somewhere. If feelings do not come out straight, they end up doing me, and possibly others, more harm in the long run. Today I interpret those expressions to mean I do not want to "hang on" to the pain of these feelings but I need to be honest with myself and another person if I want to go on functioning in a healthy way.

MEDITATION FOR TODAY

I ask that You help me to face my feelings honestly and share them with another human being.

TODAY I WILL REMEMBER

Avoiding feelings is not a sign of either wellness or of working the Program.

September 7

Often I want to break away from all of my responsibilities. These are some of my choices: I can become hot with frustration and anger, attacking those I love, crushing them (and I will feel remorse).

OR

I can sigh, crushing myself with the weight of inadequacy or resignation or the futility of it all (and I will waste time and feel guilty).

OR

I can STOP now, stand aside for a moment, and look and listen. I will see I am heaping abuse upon myself, inflicting it because once again I have not done enough. Or I will feel fear; fear that I might be like that person who is bugging me so much. So I must LOOK AT MYSELF WITH KINDNESS, and tell myself to keep it simple. Then I can pick myself up and begin again, taking another step, an even surer one toward knowing who I am.

MEDITATION FOR TODAY

Oh, God, help me to know I have a choice.

TODAY I WILL REMEMBER

I will go easier on myself and look at myself with kindness.

September 8

REFLECTION FOR TODAY

In trying to change into being the person I want to be, I ask myself what kind of people I most enjoy being with. I like to be around others who have a sense of humor, who can laugh at themselves, and giggle at life's peculiarities. I enjoy those who are considerate of others' feelings, who are happy, and comfortable to be with. I admire people who are positive in their thinking and who are even-tempered. I can become this kind of person by developing these qualities and characteristics. I must build on my assets concentrating on the positive factors of my personality. I must ask my Higher Power for help to believe in me.

MEDITATION FOR TODAY

Help me to be the kind of person whose company I enjoy.

TODAY I WILL REMEMBER

The going is slow but I have all my life to work on this growth.

September 9

REFLECTION FOR TODAY

When we begin to open ourselves to living, we generally feel a great deal of freedom. Yet we are also aware of our fear. Suddenly many choices lie before us. Of course we do not want to make a mistake which may hurt us later. But we do not want to miss out any longer either. Like a new colt out in the pasture for the first time, we are apt to stumble and fall.

MEDITATION FOR TODAY

May I be patient with myself when I make a mistake. Mistakes can be unexpected learning experiences.

TODAY I WILL REMEMBER

It does not matter how many times I stumble and fall; it matters only that I pick myself up, learn, and go forward.

September 10

REFLECTION FOR TODAY

Most of my life situations call for a response, one which is a choice between love and power. I can react either in a loving, compassionate manner, or I can choose to exercise my power by demanding, intimidating, manipulating, or attempting to influence in a way which is beneficial to me. Giving advice to others can be an attempt to control. Giving to others what I want them to have is not necessarily a loving act.

MEDITATION FOR TODAY

Loving well is a learned behavior which requires effort and time. Help me to be a good student.

TODAY I WILL REMEMBER

Loving is a choice.

September 11

REFLECTION FOR TODAY

Learning to love ourselves is possibly our greatest task. For most of us to really care for ourselves and to become vulnerable takes a very long time. We struggle so often with the knowledge of our inadequacies, fear, guilt, and shame. We tell ourselves, "I will never be accepted if I tell her this....I will accept myself when..." We cannot put off acceptance until we meet criteria for ourselves. Likely that time will never come. We need to accept ourselves, right now, with our weaknesses. Our weaknesses, when faced, will lead us to untapped strength. And we never will truly gain someone's acceptance unless we risk being vulnerable.

MEDITATION FOR TODAY

With Your help, I will accept myself today, just as I am.

TODAY I WILL REMEMBER

Acceptance and love go hand in hand. Because I am loveable, I can love someone and I can accept love.

September 12

In the process of learning and growing, I often find myself needing to deal with something I thought I had already eliminated. At these times I have rejected myself for being where I was. "I should not be here again," I thought. Slowly I am gaining the humility to understand that the Program offers me greater and greater levels of healing. We only have to be willing to meet with honesty the challenges which confront us for healing and growth to continue.

MEDITATION FOR TODAY

Thank You for the opportunity You give me to heal more deeply and to experience life in all its abundance.

TODAY I WILL REMEMBER

I will continue healing and growing; I will become freer and freer.

September 13

We learn in EA that we are powerless over our feelings. If we are feeling depressed or anxious, we cannot command ourselves to feel better. We have been given a set of Steps for sane living. When following these instructions we begin to feel better. We may not be able to control our feelings, but we do have the power to act. We can follow the Program by working the Steps. Sometimes we may be "doing good" but "feeling bad." We are doing what we think God would have us do and still feel depressed or anxious. Our experience in EA shows us that if we persevere, sooner or later our feelings catch up with our actions. Our Step work pays off and we feel good again.

MEDITATION FOR TODAY

Help me remember that positive thoughts and actions can improve feelings.

TODAY I WILL REMEMBER

Nothing changes unless something changes.

September 14

REFLECTION FOR TODAY

Many people I meet in the course of my life will not like me. This fact does not have to affect my self-worth and dignity as a person. Some people will be unable to like me because of their own problems. I can have serenity knowing that God and I believe I am a worthwhile person. Since I know I am always loved by God, I do not need to be overly concerned with other peoples' perceptions of me. It would be nice if we all liked one another, but that is not the real world.

MEDITATION FOR TODAY

Help me to realize my self-worth and dignity as a person.

TODAY I WILL REMEMBER

I do not need to be approved, liked, or loved by everyone.

September 15

REFLECTION FOR TODAY

For years I ran from pain thinking denial would make it go away. But denying the pain only created more and more anguish and isolation. Hearing the phrase, "Pain is inevitable, suffering is optional" touched the core of my being. The reality is that as a human being I will experience pain. It is inevitable. Knowing I can alleviate needless suffering if I am willing to risk facing my pain creates a feeling of hope and security in me.

MEDITATION FOR TODAY

Help me to face my pain. Give me the courage to share my hurts with another for it will rid me of my isolation.

TODAY I WILL REMEMBER

Feeling pain is a sign that I am human, open to life, and growing.

September 16

REFLECTION FOR TODAY

At times I need to feel appreciated. I need "strokes" which tell me I did a good job or I am a good person. These approvals do not always come when they are most needed. Those are the times when I must appreciate myself. It is hard for me to acknowledge my own worth. But how can anybody else appreciate me if I do not appreciate me? It is right for me to have pride in myself. It is right for me to like myself. Not only is it right, it is absolutely necessary.

MEDITATION FOR TODAY

Dear God, help me to realize I am truly a special person - not only to others - but to me.

TODAY I WILL REMEMBER

I am better than okay.

September 17

REFLECTION FOR TODAY

Thinking back over some crises in my life, one common thread seems to run through them. I emerged a little bit stronger, a little bit wiser, and a little more appreciative of the ways and methods of my Higher Power. I now realize that each incident presented me with two different choices: negative - I could crawl under a rock and curl up and die; positive - I could accept it as an opportunity for change with a new attitude toward an old, familiar situation. What really impressed me was that the choice was mine. It was up to me to decide which direction I wanted to take and which attitude I wanted to adopt. If there was doubt in my mind, I turned it over to my Higher Power.

MEDITATION FOR TODAY

May I continue to look at crises as an opportunity to grow.

TODAY I WILL REMEMBER

My choice will be positive.

September 18

REFLECTION FOR TODAY

In the past there were so many things I had to do, planned to do, or needed to do. When I thought of tackling any of these things, I ended up doing nothing but my usual reading, sleeping, or daydreaming and then had to think up excuses why nothing had been accomplished. I made fervent promises that tomorrow I would really get to it and get it all done. I knew full well the list was endless and that tomorrow would contain even more things to do; more than I could reasonably accomplish in one day. I am now trying to make a conscious effort to do at least one thing on this list which I do not want to do and I have stopped making excuses.

MEDITATION FOR TODAY

May I make the conscious effort to start my day with the God of my understanding asking for strength and courage to take action.

TODAY I WILL REMEMBER

I will make an effort to do at least one thing I really do not want to do.

September 19

Short term relief is all I get when I run away and hide from my problems. Whatever shield or defense mechanism I use to hide behind eventually becomes too burdensome. It becomes greater than the problem. When I run from pain in a personal relationship, I may lose the chance to cultivate a deep and meaningful friendship. Working at friendship helps me weather the ups and downs of relationships. Running from a problem at work could take away an opportunity to find solutions to problems. Hiding in the back of the room at an EA meeting takes away my opportunity to share. Running from conflict does not produce a winner - just a loser: ME.

MEDITATION FOR TODAY

Help me to find the strength to confront whatever I want to run away from.

TODAY I WILL REMEMBER

To run out is to hide out; to hide out is to lose out.

September 20

Prospective changes in my life used to fill me with panic, especially major changes such as jobs, homes, or relationships. Major upheavals in one's life are never easy but I have learned now to trust my Higher Power. I have learned to be more relaxed when anticipating changes. I no longer believe the worst scenario will be playing out in my life. There have been so many examples of good coming to me through changes which I dreaded. When we had to leave a beloved home, our whole lifestyle changed in a delightful manner. A job change I did not want turned into a fascinating challenge. I know many whose lives have changed incredibly for the better after an unwanted divorce. Change is growth if we accept it.

MEDITATION FOR TODAY

I thank You for the good which will come with the changes in my life.

TODAY I WILL REMEMBER

I only need to trust in my Higher Power and welcome change.

September 21

We may think we have many friends but if we have two or three, we are richly blessed. A test of friendship could be if we were arrested for some terrible crime, would that person still be there to support us? How many of our friends would actually meet this criteria? If we have a friend who gives us this kind of acceptance, we would be wise to value that relationship. How accepting am I of my own human nature? Do I see that I am capable of doing anything anyone else might do? If I see that I can, I will be more capable of giving this kind of acceptance.

MEDITATION FOR TODAY

Help me to be the kind of friend I would like to have.

TODAY I WILL REMEMBER

I will be conscious of my needs, as well as the needs of those I love, for unconditional acceptance.

September 22

This morning I see the sun is not shining. That can contribute to my being a crab today if I let it. By noon I realize that the reason the day is not being much fun is because I am teeing off on people and situations around me. To become aware of myself in that situation seems to require a jolt - someone coming back at me in such a way that tells me to shove off, to quit being a problem person. And even then I sometimes tell myself it is okay to be a crab. The difficult part is sorting out when I am the problem or the other person is.

MEDITATION FOR TODAY

Help me not to be a problem person. Help me to know when I need to stand firm for my position. I want to learn how to tell the difference.

TODAY I WILL REMEMBER

To at least make an attempt to sort things out, to tell the difference, then act on the decision.

September 23

REFLECTION FOR TODAY

I am a guilt addict! The Twelve Step Program is helping me to recover from this addiction. Slowly my eyes are opening to the truth of my behavior and how it feeds this addiction. In the past I would overfill each day with "must dos" and "have tos" and "shoulds" so that each evening I felt exhausted and guilty about what did not get done. Each morning began with leftover guilt feelings from the behavior of the day before. The future appeared as a repeat of the past: not enough time for the perfect performance of every duty and desire. By practicing the Program I have become aware of my addiction and the harm it does me. This awareness is followed by acceptance, forgiveness, and then action.

MEDITATION FOR TODAY

Help me concentrate on Step Three today. This Step ever reminds me that Your will for me does not have a guilt "aftertaste".

TODAY I WILL REMEMBER

Feeling guilty is an indulgence which always hurts me and destroys my enjoyment of the present day. I will choose to be free of it.

September 24

REFLECTION FOR TODAY

In order to maintain this loving attitude which I have started to experience, I frequently have to give up some unnecessary characteristic of my self-will. Each time it is a different item: an attitude, an erroneous belief, an unrealistic goal, or another person's approval. Once I discover through one of the Twelve Steps what is hampering my progress, I ask God to remove that defect, just for today. Steps Four and Ten are most useful when I feel separate from God and do not realize why. Working Step Four releases me from all past wrongdoings and Step Ten keeps present wrongdoings from piling up.

MEDITATION FOR TODAY

Let me not stray too far from You before I begin to work a Step to help myself.

TODAY I WILL REMEMBER

To change the things I can.

September 25

Electricity is a power greater than myself. Gravity is also a power greater than myself. I cannot control them; yet, knowing their laws, I can tap into them and put them to use for myself. From acceptance of these large, natural powers, I was able to grow into a concept of a spiritual power greater than myself. This power is the natural spiritual law. If I put my faith and trust into that power, I tap something strong and useful to my growth, both internally and externally.

MEDITATION FOR TODAY

May I take time daily by prayer and meditation to tap into Your source of limitless wisdom and love.

TODAY I WILL REMEMBER

I will let my Higher Power be my spiritual reservoir.

September 26

Learning to use the letters H-O-W has made me see things with a different perspective. Honesty -Open-Mindedness - Willingness have helped change my life in so many unexpected ways. My days are almost always good. There are a few bad days yet but those bad days are so much better than what I used to call my good days the change is remarkable. It is a pleasure to start a new day because life is great. Certainly there are stresses, but I have learned HOW to cope.

MEDITATION FOR TODAY

Never let me forget how useful HOW is.

TODAY I WILL REMEMBER

How it used to be before HOW.

September 27

How often have we dwelt on feeling sad, lonely, inadequate, guilty, or shameful and wondered why we felt so miserable? Once we are able to look behind our feelings to our thinking, we quickly see the messages we had been sending to ourselves were the reason for feeling so miserable and unhappy. We can choose to stop talking to ourselves critically. Who we are and what we feel is okay. In fact, we need to be right where we are. We can only grow from that place. Accepting ourselves as we are will bring us to the next step of our journey.

MEDITATION FOR TODAY

Help me to recognize when I am "picking" on me.

TODAY I WILL REMEMBER

I will choose to talk lovingly to myself in response to my feelings.

September 28

REFLECTION FOR TODAY

One of the many tools I have learned to use since coming to the Program is that of writing things down. I am always surprised at how much I write. If I am unable to sleep at night, I get up and write. It certainly is better than tossing and turning in bed. If something is bothering me during the day and I do not know what it is, I write and write some more. It is like my Higher Power is guiding my hand. I do not know what I am going to write until I see what I have written. It is amazing how many problems can be solved just by seeing them spelled out in black and white.

MEDITATION FOR TODAY

May I always remember that writing things down helps me to see them more clearly.

TODAY I WILL REMEMBER

If I can see the problem, I can find a way to solve it.

September 29

Before joining the Program, I often thought I would really be happy if a certain situation worked out to my advantage. I anticipated great benefits if my plans worked out. When I did not get what I wanted, I was full of self-pity, saying constantly, "If only..." When I got what I wanted, I often still felt disappointed when I realized my unrealistically high expectations would not be met. As I have grown in the Program, I have learned to have more realistic expectations. Where I used to expect great benefits, I am now grateful for small improvements. Where I used to feel self-pity, I now feel more serenity in knowing my true happiness comes from being at peace with myself.

MEDITATION FOR TODAY

Help me to know more serenity by better maintaining a realistic perspective concerning the results of my efforts.

TODAY I WILL REMEMBER

It can be a long fall from high expectations.

September 30

REFLECTION FOR TODAY

Negative or unpleasant emotions are not a yardstick of reality, or of my self-worth. Because I feel shame, for instance, does not mean I should be ashamed of myself. Because I feel panic does not necessarily mean there is something to be afraid of. Feelings may have no external or intellectual significance. Feelings are meant to be experienced and accepted - not analyzed. All I can conclude from feeling bad is that I am feeling bad. I realize that emotions are neither good nor bad; that feelings do not make me a good or bad person; that emotions and intellect are separate. Trying to "interpret" the intellectual meaning of my emotions is useless - like trying to spell words but using only numbers.

MEDITATION FOR TODAY

Help me to accept my feelings without judging them or myself.

TODAY I WILL REMEMBER

My best strategy in dealing with unpleasant emotions is simple acceptance.

October

October 1

REFLECTION FOR TODAY

I remember being so full of hate for someone that I ran movies in my head about committing violence against them. My hate produced envy, spite, and rage. Now I have learned through the Twelve Steps that I can and must forgive for my own mental health. And if I am unable to forgive, I can pray for my adversary. As long as I allow the hate to dominate my thoughts, that hate is running my life and there is no opportunity for my Higher Power to enter.

MEDITATION FOR TODAY

May I remember today to pray for those who I find hard to love.

TODAY I WILL REMEMBER

Today I will practice forgiveness.

October 2

REFLECTION FOR TODAY

So many of my negative feelings stem from carrying feelings from the past into today, or from projecting what might go wrong in the future. I do this every time I expect difficulty, failure, or rejection. I am pulling out my past pain and wearing it all over again. I do it, too, when I start thinking during a moment of pleasure, "it won't work out like this again." When I remember to enjoy each moment for the sheer delight and goodness it offers, when I look upon negative experiences as lessons for improving my life, I am cutting my life into manageable proportions.

MEDITATION FOR TODAY

With Your help, may I make the most of each moment.

TODAY I WILL REMEMBER

I will live this day as fully as I can and, at the end of the day, I will let it go.

October 3

REFLECTION FOR TODAY

It is part of my emotional illness that I feel a vague but overwhelming sense of something wrong with me. If allowed to control me, this feeling leads to withdrawal, despondency, and a sense of powerlessness. The antidote is self-acceptance. This does not mean that I deny my shortcomings. In a searching and fearless inventory I honestly recognize my defects and my good points. If I set a goal of eliminating all the defects, I am doomed to failure. Only by accepting and using my positive qualities can I develop the strength to reduce the defects.

MEDITATION FOR TODAY

Help me to concentrate on my strengths.

TODAY I WILL REMEMBER

What I am is God's gift to me. What I make of myself is my gift to God.

October 4

REFLECTION FOR TODAY

Often I look back and say, "I knew better than to do that." I knew before I used the angry word, blamed, shouted, ran away, etc. that what I was doing was wrong. I did it anyway. Now with a daily program and a planned quiet time I can avoid many of these backward looks by realizing when the danger signs appear. I can choose at that time how to handle these situations. I can avoid hurting others through a daily Step Ten. I can really acknowledge the feelings as mine and choose how to handle them during a quiet time.

MEDITATION FOR TODAY

Let me keep an eye out for danger signs and seek quiet when they arise.

TODAY I WILL REMEMBER

Only in quiet can I hear my inner voice and make a choice.

October 5

REFLECTION FOR TODAY

Live and let live reminds me that my first responsibility is to myself. I must take care of myself the way my Higher Power wants me to. When I can accept myself, it becomes easier to accept others. When I allow myself to be myself, I am able to let others be themselves. This creates a lovely balance between others and me. When I take responsibility for myself I lose my need to control others.

MEDITATION FOR TODAY

You made me the way I am and my job is to accept me and live with me to the best of my ability.

TODAY I WILL REMEMBER

If I focus on making this day as good as it can be for me, I will not have time to worry about others.

October 6

Pain had been the motivator for me to come into the Program. After some time, the pain lessened in intensity and frequency. When I felt good and happy, I thought I did not need the Program any more. These thoughts scared me so I began to create pain and misery for myself so I would be motivated to work the Program. I became frightened of being happy and serene. I am learning that the desire to live a better life is a sufficient motivator. The pain which brought me here can be transformed into the gratitude which keeps me here.

MEDITATION FOR TODAY

May I remember that as I grow in the Program, my values and perspectives will change.

TODAY I WILL REMEMBER

Flexibility in my thinking enables me to go with rather than against the changes God has in store for me.

October 7

REFLECTION FOR TODAY

Being afraid of rejection, I did not trust sharing my honest feelings. Trusting seemed so scary but once I understood the only way to let go of the fear of rejection was by my trusting, I became more willing to take the risk. As I took the risk to share and was accepted, my willingness to risk grew. The more I shared the more acceptance I received; the more acceptance I received, the more trust I developed.

MEDITATION FOR TODAY

At times I feel so scared, God. Help me to risk sharing the parts of myself I want to run from the most.

TODAY I WILL REMEMBER

Trust builds from the action of risking.

October 8

REFLECTION FOR TODAY

There are many important words involved in our Program but two of the most important are humility and responsibility. Much of my progress can be measured by these two words. They are extremely hard for me to accept and use. Humility bothers me because it goes against the grain of my false pride. Responsibility is tough because it is so much easier to let someone else take care of things. When I am responsible, I take care of my commitments and obligations. Most times that is hard work. When I accept and practice humility and responsibility, I grow rapidly.

MEDITATION FOR TODAY

It is hard to be humble and responsible. Please ease my way.

TODAY I WILL REMEMBER

Humility and responsibility equal maturity and manageability.

October 9

REFLECTION FOR TODAY

Am I so important I am the only one who can do things for others? I used to believe the world was falling apart because I was *becoming* incapable of handling every *thing*. My need to be needed was so strong I felt everything depended on me and me alone. Ego, pride, and self-will had me in their grip. I have come to realize that real help comes from allowing others to learn to do for themselves. I am now stepping back and letting others learn from their own mistakes as we all have to do.

MEDITATION FOR TODAY

Help me to love, but not to take over.

TODAY I WILL REMEMBER

I will allow others to do what they have to do.

October 10

I often ask my Higher Power to help me know what is best for me. And often I hear my Higher Power answer and know in my heart it is best and yet I do nothing. Then I punish myself because I have asked and have received, yet have taken no action. In fact, the knowledge of what is best for me often causes me great anxiety and my fear overwhelms what I know. I have been given knowledge but have not asked for courage as well. Knowledge is a wonderful gift, but I accomplish little if I do not have the courage to act.

MEDITATION FOR TODAY

Higher Power, grant me courage as well as knowledge.

TODAY I WILL REMEMBER

I need all my Higher Power's gifts.

October 11

My outside appearance is a good indication of how I feel inside. When my inside emotional stability is running amok, it is time to start getting the outside in order first. Are my clothes clean? Do they need repairs? Is my hair combed and washed and does it need cutting or curling? How about a long, hot bath or shower? When was the last time I visited the dentist or had a good physical from my doctor? I need to make certain my emotional difficulties are not aggravated by a physical ailment such as allergies, blood sugar fluctuations, or chemical imbalances. Now that I am refreshed and looking good, I can call some friends for coffee or lunch or I can have people come over to my place for a visit. Doing these things can help to change my attitude.

MEDITATION FOR TODAY

My body houses the soul You gave me. Help me to keep it in good working condition.

TODAY I WILL REMEMBER

Taking care of myself means physically, mentally, and emotionally.

October 12

REFLECTION FOR TODAY

I am glad to realize that, while I cannot will away negative feelings such as fear, anger, or despair, I need not be ruled by them. No matter how overpowering my emotions may be, I can focus on something which will feed my serenity. Although strong feelings may blind this fact, the world is full of goodness and beauty. As surely as I can be upset by any person, place, or things, I can find better experiences to enjoy.

MEDITATION FOR TODAY

May I reflect on everything in my life which brings me happiness or serenity.

TODAY I WILL REMEMBER

Why would I choose to respond to something negative when I can respond to something positive?

October 13

When I am feeling especially lonely, the pain inside makes me wonder why I have to go through this. The longer I am in the Program and share my pain, the more I am aware that others hurt also. This common bond helps me to understand, care, and grow. Pain is nature's way of telling me I have a need which has to be taken care of whether it is physical or emotional. I need to take care of myself and I can do it.

MEDITATION FOR TODAY

Help me to realize my pain is worthwhile because it draws me closer to You and to others and it gives me compassion.

TODAY I WILL REMEMBER

Whenever I share my pain, someone comes into my life with a similar pain to remind me I am not alone.

October 14

REFLECTION FOR TODAY

I would like to reflect a minute on the changing seasons. I live in a cold climate, cold in winter, and I have decided I want to stay; not retire to the "Sunbelt". I certainly do not have anything against warm climates. What the winter does for me is to let things rest for a while, including perhaps my spirit. I cannot possibly grow all the time. Perhaps if I stop and rest occasionally - in the "winter" of my soul - and be quiet, which is very hard for me to do, the growth will resume in the "spring" of my soul. And perhaps my growth will be greater and more assured.

MEDITATION FOR TODAY

Because it is difficult for me to rest, to slow down, or to meditate, help me to allow myself the freedom to do so.

TODAY I WILL REMEMBER

Progress is not always a high-speed freeway. I need to remember to pull in, shut off the motor, and rest my spirit.

October 15

REFLECTION FOR TODAY

Someone said at a meeting that anger comes from other people not meeting my expectations. If that is true, and I see it is true for me, then I have two choices. I can either stay angry or I can lower my expectations. If I choose to stay angry, the only person I hurt is myself. My blood pressure goes up, I get acid indigestion, headaches, and become depressed. Or I can choose to lower my expectations. That is another way of letting go of what I cannot control, of not playing God by thinking that my way is the only right way.

MEDITATION FOR TODAY

I ask You to help me deal with my anger honestly.

TODAY I WILL REMEMBER

Unrealistic expectations for myself or others creates anger.

October 16

REFLECTION FOR TODAY

Because I was so impatient and critical of myself, gaining compassion was not an easy task. Now as I talk kindly to myself instead of critically, I gain more and more compassion for myself. When I am gentle with myself, I feel peace inside even in the midst of turmoil. When I am gentle with myself, I become gentle with others. It is this gentleness and caring, not impatience and criticism, which brings about continued growth and healing.

MEDITATION FOR TODAY

When I resist being kind to myself, may I recall that compassion precedes growth.

TODAY I WILL REMEMBER

I no longer need to hate me.

October 17

Resigning as Master of the Universe was a relief and a weight off of my shoulders. The world can actually revolve without me. Now I can concentrate on the people around me. Instead of doing all the talking, I can do more listening. Instead of giving orders, I can ask for other peoples' opinions on how things should be done. Well, God, it is all Yours. Isn't that a simple way to handle a difficult problem? If I can't handle it, God can if I just ask. The delicious sense of relief, a relaxing effect on the body, and a quietness of the mind are just a few of the results which are mine from this simple turning it over.

MEDITATION FOR TODAY

Thank You, God, for always having Your shoulder ready for me to lean on.

TODAY I WILL REMEMBER

God will carry the load.

October 18

REFLECTION FOR TODAY

Something to reach for, something to work toward, a reason to get out of bed in the morning, or a purpose for taking care of myself physically, mentally, and emotionally. They all add up to GOAL. When I was in an emotional upheaval, goals were something which other people had. People with education, looks, money, and talent. But certainly not me. I did not realize goals were personal guidelines which I could use to improve the quality of my life. Any part of my life that needs to be changed is an opportunity for goal setting. Physically I could have a weight loss goal, a quit smoking goal, or a physical fitness goal. Mentally I could have a goal to change an attitude, a goal to broaden my interests and increase my knowledge, or a goal to read a good book every week. Emotionally my goal is for serenity which can be gained by learning to live and let live and to roll with the punches.

MEDITATION FOR TODAY

Help me see a real need for change and to pick a goal and go for it.

TODAY I WILL REMEMBER

The only thing keeping me from reaching a goal is me.

October 19

My being a doormat came from a need in my emotional illness; a need for recognition and approval from others. In recovery, I began to recognize my own power to determine my self-worth. I no longer use what others will think of me as a guide for how I will act. I look within myself for my standards of behavior and seek the will of my Higher Power in all matters. I am beginning to take responsibility for my own life. Part of this responsibility is making my own choices and accepting the consequences.

MEDITATION FOR TODAY

Grant me the ability to look at my own power to affect other people.

TODAY I WILL REMEMBER

How much do I react to the power I perceive in other people?

October 20

The Slogan "Know Thyself - Be Honest" makes me aware of how often I ignore my feelings or try to rationalize them away. If I am to know myself, I must acknowledge my emotions just as they are. It may be I am letting a past experience creep in to distort my reaction to a situation. Or perhaps I am allowing old inferior feelings to cause me pain. I may be holding back feelings related directly to a present situation because it is easier (or so it seems) than having to confront, express, or risk rejection.

MEDITATION FOR TODAY

Help me to work at honestly knowing myself, day by day, minute by minute.

TODAY I WILL REMEMBER

The pain of facing my feelings is far less than the pain of suppressing them.

October 21

REFLECTION FOR TODAY

It is not humanly possible to "like" every person with whom we come in contact. There will always be people who will say or do things with which we will disagree. It is probable that we affect others the same way. No one is exactly like anyone else. The differences make for a variety in our life and should be as welcome as the different varieties of flowers in our gardens. All of us, regardless of our race, beliefs, color, or ethnic background, were created by a loving God. It is not necessary to "like" everyone - only to accept them.

MEDITATION FOR TODAY

Thank You for the differences in people which truly spices up the adventure of living.

TODAY I WILL REMEMBER

We each take our own special road toward the same spiritual quest.

October 22

Given the same set of circumstances, we can do anything anyone else can do: steal, kill, write bad checks, or commit adultery. If we think we are above such behavior, we are naive. How readily can we accept that we are as capable of doing anything anyone else could do? For those of us who have been sheltered, it may take a bit longer to discover just how close we can come to any of these behaviors. We are fortunate, indeed, if we come to a point where we are forced to at least face one of these aspects of our personality. Once we see how capable we are of doing a particular thing we may not have believed possible, we gain a deeper acceptance of our own humanity. Our freedom increases. In turn, we accept others more easily.

MEDITATION FOR TODAY

May I be open to the reality of my own humanness.

TODAY I WILL REMEMBER

Accepting ourselves helps us accept others, too.

October 23

Too often I let external things distract me when someone is speaking at a meeting. Maybe dirty fingernails, a wrong color of lipstick, or length of hair or beard will affect my concentration. Maybe a person's poor grammar will have me making corrections in my mind instead of listening to the thoughts and feelings being expressed. Often when I really listen I really learn. I know my Higher Power works through people and, if I don't hear people, I won't hear God either. My progress in my recovery depends on learning from other people. I have no right to be critical or judgemental of others.

MEDITATION FOR TODAY

Open my mind to the shared suggestions of others. Remind me that externals are not important.

TODAY I WILL REMEMBER

I am no better or worse than anyone else.

October 24

REFLECTION FOR TODAY

Intimacy is being soft together. Many of you have observed the intimacy of a new relationship. It appeared exciting and wonderful. Yet this stage of the relationship ultimately passes. The conflict stage creeps in. Are we willing to deal with this stage or do we run? Only after we face our conflict head on can we come to experience the kind of intimacy and caring in a relationship which nurtures us and pushes us to become all we can be.

MEDITATION FOR TODAY

May I have the courage to deal with conflict realizing that dealing with it will raise my self-esteem.

TODAY I WILL REMEMBER

The more acceptance I have for myself, the more intimacy I will be capable of experiencing.

October 25

REFLECTION FOR TODAY

Hate is a strong, controlling force if carried to the utmost degree. Oftentimes I will say I hate a person when in reality I only dislike what the person does. If I hate with a vengeance, the destructiveness of this emotion can invade every avenue of my daily life. The responses I give others become vindictive. The successes I win are most likely at the expense and mercy of others. The world in which I live becomes a disagreeable place rather than comforting. The spite I feel becomes my sole motive for living. My physical body becomes susceptible to pain and illnesses, which need not be. My obsession with hate hides the ability of my seeing I am doing harm to myself.

MEDITATION FOR TODAY

Help me to recognize my own destructive behavior caused by the hatred felt toward another human being. Give me courage to differ with others without doing harm to them or to myself. Guide me to become a more forgiving and accepting person.

TODAY I WILL REMEMBER

I choose to replace hatred with love and understanding.

October 26

REFLECTION FOR TODAY

The more we are able to embrace our sorrow and learn from it, the more we will also be capable of experiencing great joy. Yet to embrace our sorrow takes a great deal of courage. So often we try to soften or resist our pain. In every painful situation there is a lesson to be learned. Our willingness to be open to this learning ultimately brings us to experience a greater joy than we had believed possible.

MEDITATION FOR TODAY

May I hang on during my painful times, knowing my pain will eventually turn again into joy.

TODAY I WILL REMEMBER

The depth of my sorrow mirrors the peak of my joy.

October 27

REFLECTION FOR TODAY

I really feel great when someone lets me know they appreciate me. In thinking about that, I realized how often I feel appreciative of others and do not express that feeling in words. I seem to take it for granted they will know my feelings without hearing them. This applies to all the people I deal with: my spouse, my children, co-workers, and salespeople, for example. From my own experiences I know that just to know one is appreciated can mean a great deal. On this day I will express my appreciation. I will let others know how much they mean to me and how I admire and am grateful for their efforts. I will be certain to include members of my family, who usually bear the brunt of my criticisms.

MEDITATION FOR TODAY

May I remember that to someone who is feeling discouraged, appreciation can make the difference between giving up and holding on.

TODAY I WILL REMEMBER

Appreciate - not denigrate!

October 28

We never fail until we quit trying. The battle is never over until we win or quit. Often we are tempted in times of distress to become discouraged and throw up our hands in defeat. Discouragement is actually a clue to make us pause and see what needs to be changed. It is time to pray for direction and then try and try again. Usually it is easier to quit, but how proud we are, and have a right to be, when we stick to it and win our personal "war".

MEDITATION FOR TODAY

Help us to keep on keeping on even when the going is tough.

TODAY I WILL REMEMBER

Never quit trying!

October 29

REFLECTION FOR TODAY

I awaken this day with the faith that there will be enough time to accomplish all that is necessary. As I think of the tasks ahead, I do not concentrate on how many there are or how long they might take. I know my Higher Power is with me in all my undertakings. I can start each job calmly, believing God will aid me in my work and the tasks will be accomplished in the right manner and at the right time. My hands and mind will be guided all day. When the work is done for the day, there will be time for play.

MEDITATION FOR TODAY

Thank You for Your guidance throughout this day in the completion of my appointed tasks.

TODAY I WILL REMEMBER

Anything is possible with God's help.

October 30

REFLECTION FOR TODAY

Loneliness is a feeling many of us do not want to admit having. Perhaps our false pride stops us. It is hard to acknowledge we could be at a huge party and still be lonely. Few of us who are married or have significant others want our friends to realize it is possible to be lonely even in a strong relationship. And yet we must not hold this feeling in. It is, after all, part of our saying, HALT, which warns us never to let ourselves get too: hungry, angry, lonely, or tired. It can be dangerous for us not to share our loneliness. Let us break down the pride barrier and call a friend today. Maybe that friend is lonely also.

MEDITATION FOR TODAY

Grant me the courage to accept and express my loneliness.

TODAY I WILL REMEMBER

Reach out for comfort.

October 31

Halloween - The traditional day for disguises and masquerades. Most of my life I have been wearing masks and showing a phony facade to the world. Much of the time pride has been at the root of this deception (self-deception as well) usually disguising itself as a virtue. I have a never-ending job of uncovering pride daily so it does not push me backward. Forward is the way I want to go. Pride hides my faults from me and keeps me from helping others, as well as myself. It slows my growth and gives me a false sense of security.

MEDITATION FOR TODAY

I pray I can be realistic enough to accept my assets without being proud.

TODAY I WILL REMEMBER

I am through with masks and masquerading - except at Halloween parties.

November

November 1

REFLECTION FOR TODAY

Can atheists be at home in EA? Yes. I found the Program when my self-willed ways had emptied out and I was nearly set to turn it over. Nature was my ready choice for higher power. But in my Fourth Step I learned I was addicted to nature for relief from social pain. So I turned to mankind, asking that our connections be restored. Probably my higher power will change further, but it is certain that my bonds with mankind *and* nature are sounder now - and more spiritual. I am becoming a better atheist!

MEDITATION FOR TODAY

May self-will never again prevent me from see-ing what a small thing a difference of ideas is in the spiritual adventure we share.

TODAY I WILL REMEMBER

Turning it over works. I will turn it over, then wonder to what, if I must.

November 2

REFLECTION FOR TODAY

Yesterday I had a "slip". I let my feelings run amok. Feelings I had not felt for a long time surfaced. It frightened me to realize these feelings are still with me and that I have not been "cured". I must remember it is human to have lapses and to concern myself with doing well today and not worrying about yesterday. Feeling guilty does not make me noble or solve any of my problems. Guilt only drags me down.

MEDITATION FOR TODAY

May I forgive myself, as I know You have forgiven me.

TODAY I WILL REMEMBER

Human feelings are okay for me to have because I am human, thank God.

November 3

REFLECTION FOR TODAY

A river cannot be rerouted successfully without making a new channel *and* damming up the old one. If you put the dam up without a new channel being ready, the water may or may not go where you want it to. It may cause flooding or break the dam or it many rechannel itself into an undesired place. So it is with our habits. If we stop an old habit without being ready to (usually because someone tells us to), we chance failing and getting discouraged. We chance forming other undesirable habits. We chance getting ourselves so discouraged we give up.

MEDITATION FOR TODAY

Remind me that progress takes time and patience.

TODAY I WILL REMEMBER

My habits were not formed overnight. I need to give myself time to replace negative traits with positive traits.

November 4

REFLECTION FOR TODAY

It is not easy to admit I am powerless over my emotions. After all, I would not be this way if everyone or everything were not like they are. After all, I am able to keep my emotions suppressed inside me. After all, I *should* feel the way I do. But, it is an honest Program. I must admit my anger lasts too long and is too severe. My depression is too deep and immobilizing. My fear is too overwhelming and ever present. I have tried to handle these feelings, but I am unable to. I do not control them. They control me. Indeed, I am powerless over my emotions.

MEDITATION FOR TODAY

Help me to remember that powerlessness is a condition - not a feeling.

TODAY I WILL REMEMBER

I am powerless over my emotions!

November 5

There are so many ways I can be helpful to others. When I am feeling sorry for myself, I will try to remember what I can do. For example:

I can be a friend to someone who feels friendless.

I can make a call to someone I am concerned about.

I can share love with someone who feels unloved.

I can *just* listen to someone who needs to talk.

I can be *with* someone who is lonely.

I can send a cheery card to someone who is ill or having a rough time.

I can comfort someone who has lost a loved one.

I can share my experiences with someone who is confused.

None of these things take more than a little effort and yet they can accomplish wonders.

MEDITATION FOR TODAY
Let me help myself by helping others.

TODAY I WILL REMEMBER
It takes so little to do so much.

November 6

REFLECTION FOR TODAY

For a good part of my life it seemed people were always telling me to grow up. But no one ever told me where my "up" was. No one had a plan to offer for my life. I used to wonder when I would be mature. Now I know that maturity is not a place or destination. It is a never ending road in this life. I can usually look back and see the progress I have made along this road. With the help of my Higher Power and the Twelve Steps of EA, I know I will continue to mature. I am growing into a much deeper awareness of who I am and why I am here.

MEDITATION FOR TODAY

Let me always remember I am growing and maturing each day in every way toward the good which is in me.

TODAY I WILL REMEMBER

I am "ripening" at the proper stages on my road to maturity.

November 7

REFLECTION FOR TODAY

There are predictable stages of growth and when we go through them we are left feeling exposed and vulnerable. In the past many of us shut down the process of growing for we did not wish to have these feelings. How lonely and bored we became while trying to remain in control. The Program has helped us see our need for growth. Now we are able to understand that feeling exposed and vulnerable is part of a healthy, healing process. We embrace our growth periods with gratitude more quickly. As we are open, we become more of what we are capable of being.

MEDITATION FOR TODAY

May I remember that to gain my own identity I must surrender my certainty.

TODAY I WILL REMEMBER

Each growth process I encounter and meet head on gives me the gifts of freedom, spontaneity, and aliveness.

November 8

When things which usually upset me don't get to me, I know I have a hold on serenity. I just need to learn how to stay serene longer, more often, and through worse situations. Usually it helps to say to myself, "How important is it?" It also helps to be realistic about the situation, what is fair to expect, and what I can change. I also need to consider that I am the one who is hurt when I get upset. Sometimes it seems to help when I get upset but only at my expense.

MEDITATION FOR TODAY

Help me to not neglect my efforts toward serenity.

TODAY I WILL REMEMBER

Serenity is my number one goal.

November 9

A key tool I have learned to use is to act "as if". It seems to give me confidence and the ability to be what I want to be. If I have to give a speech to many people and I am nervous, I act "as if" I am in complete control of myself and the speech and it goes well. If I feel someone has hurt me and I am angry, I quietly explain my feelings and then act "as if" nothing has happened and we remain friends. It helps the anger disappear. If I am worried about the future, I act "as if" everything will turn out fine and it generally does. If problems come my way and I am in turmoil over them, I act "as if" there are solutions and options and they usually appear. When I am depressed, it really works miraculously to act "as if" life is wonderful. It is!

MEDITATION FOR TODAY

Remind me to use this handy tool when I am in need of help.

TODAY I WILL REMEMBER

When I act "as if", it is.

November 10

REFLECTION FOR TODAY

Broken relationships, or painfully unhappy ones, seem to be a common problem with people; one that causes immeasurable pain. Satisfactory relationships with the opposite sex are a need shared by many. Sex itself is something which does not get talked about much at our meetings, but relationships certainly do. Good relationships have a lot to do with good sex. When we communicate our feelings we open ourselves to good relationships, which may be sexual relationships as well. In Step Four we sweep out all our trash, and then we get rid of it in Step Five. That leaves our hearts and souls clean and open to lasting relationships, and, in turn, to healthy and satisfying sex.

MEDITATION FOR TODAY

Help me to verbally communicate my feelings to the person I care about most.

TODAY I WILL REMEMBER

If I want to improve my sex life, I will be vulnerable.

November 11

I am me. I can only be me by being unwaveringly honest and above board in thought, word, and deed. I can only feel I am making progress if I open my mind and listen attentively to others, allowing them freedom of expression and action as I hope they would do for me. I can only achieve some measure of serenity by practicing tolerance, even if I do not want to. I can only be free of fear by trusting my Higher Power. I can only be at peace by sharing my burdens and joyful discoveries with others.

MEDITATION FOR TODAY

God, please give me the mental and spiritual strength to face whatever comes my way today.

TODAY I WILL REMEMBER

I am me and that is all I have to be.

November 12

REFLECTION FOR TODAY

When I have sudden changes in plans, I need to be able to adapt and not be thrown. As a controller I am somewhat rigid and easily upset by change. If I feel inadequate in the situation, it is hard to come up with "Plan B". It helps to be flexible when unexpected changes are necessary. God will help me with this if I admit it and ask for help.

MEDITATION FOR TODAY

May I see the situation as a challenge to be adequate even when faced with surprises.

TODAY I WILL REMEMBER

God knows my frailities and will help me with them when I surrender them.

November 13

A smile, a letter of remembrance or encouragement, a pat on the shoulder, or a kind word could be the very thing which someone may need to make it through the day. We need each other. We all need phone calls, letters, and listeners. Hurts need to be understood and tears need to be shared. The old bucket brigade of yesteryear is a good example of people needing people. A fire in the community brought every able-bodied person out to form a human chain from the water source to the fire. A bucket filled with water was passed from person to person until it reached its goal. Every person in the line was needed and shared the responsibility for dousing the threatening flames. We are all needed with our special talents. Without us the world brigade would miss our hands.

MEDITATION FOR TODAY

Open my heart to others' needs and close my eyes to their shortcomings.

TODAY I WILL REMEMBER

More is accomplished with a pat on the back than with a knife in the back.

November 14

REFLECTION FOR TODAY

As I have worked the Program, I have learned recovery from my emotional illness depends on developing a deep trust and sustaining faith in a Higher Power of my understanding. My misbeliefs and disbeliefs in God, developed because of past experiences and conclusions, created a vacuum of trust and faith. I had rejected God and therefore had a difficult time understanding and utilizing a spiritual approach to my emotions and my life. Looking back over my past there were several spiritual experiences in my life when I felt as if I were whole, healthy, and one with myself. I had taken down my defenses and let myself be. I was in the care of my Higher Power at these times. Do I still doubt a God of my understanding exists?

MEDITATION FOR TODAY

I have an urgent need to believe in You, God.

TODAY I WILL REMEMBER

Faith requires honesty and effort.

November 15

REFLECTION FOR TODAY

Today I will try to remember that when I feel down everything I do seems to come out wrong. When my self-pity begins to build, I will stop, rest, gather my thoughts, and ask my Higher Power for help. God reminds me there is a tomorrow and that I can begin anew by living one day at a time. It makes life much easier. Twenty-four hours are enough for anyone. Today is a new beginning; yesterday is gone, and tomorrow is hope.

MEDITATION FOR TODAY

God, never let me feel that any shortcoming of mine is greater than Your love for me. Remind me that no matter what I have done in the past, I can begin anew.

TODAY I WILL REMEMBER

I am beginning again.

November 16

REFLECTION FOR TODAY

One of the greatest benefits I have received from changing my life is the ability to really see and appreciate nature. During my unmanageable days I never looked at my surroundings. I did not care if the sun was shining or if it were raining. What a pleasure now to take a few serene moments out of a busy day to just look at the sun, blue sky, flowers, and even insects. How can I not thank my Higher Power for these creations?

MEDITATION FOR TODAY

Help me to always be thankful for the loveliness of this earth. Remind me to set aside a few minutes of my day to really look at the world around me.

TODAY I WILL REMEMBER

When life gets hectic, I will imagine myself sitting at the edge of a beautiful lake with the sun warming my body and the insects buzzing lazily around me.

November 17

How often have I said, "It is not that I am angry, but..."? Yet my actions show that anger is exactly what I feel. Our Program teaches me about feelings. I am learning one day at a time how to identify what I feel and to *stop denying* that I feel it. Feelings are natural. They tell me what is going on with me. The Program does not teach me not to feel, but how to react to my feelings. Am I still denying my feelings?

MEDITATION FOR TODAY

With Your help may I begin daily to surrender uncomfortable feelings to You.

TODAY I WILL REMEMBER

It's okay for me to feel.

November 18

REFLECTION FOR TODAY

Usually as we face and deal with shameful experiences we begin to understand why we responded the way we did. Compassion for ourselves increases and it feels so comforting. Finally we can talk to ourselves about the experiences with gentleness rather than criticism. Our gentle ways draw others to us. Through these relationships we realize even more, no matter how devastating an experience might have been in our past, once we share it, it becomes a help to someone in the present.

MEDITATION FOR TODAY

May I remember I need no longer be alone with my pain.

TODAY I WILL REMEMBER

Acceptance of my experiences gives me compassion for myself and then for others.

November 19

REFLECTION FOR TODAY

I look at myself as a person and say, "This is what I am right now." I judge myself and create an attitude, usually negative, about myself. And it is that attitude which I have toward myself that determines how other people feel about me or how they will react to me. The Program is teaching me to think about my assets rather than my liabilities. It is necessary for me to spend some quiet time daily trying to gain a more positive perspective on my life.

MEDITATION FOR TODAY

May I develop a more positive attitude about myself. Help me to stop putting myself down, which will allow me to respect me.

TODAY I WILL REMEMBER

Accentuate MY positive.

November 20

My attitude toward the pain in my life will determine how I experience it. Pain is not the worst thing which can befall me. This is worse: not being able to feel. Pain is a natural part of life, like air, breath, love, and death. It is not meant to diminish my life or me. Only if I resist it is my life made smaller and my misery increased. My happiness and my pain can live together in me.

MEDITATION FOR TODAY

Help me to accept the things I cannot change.

TODAY I WILL REMEMBER

I can enjoy my life today even though I may have emotional or physical pain.

November 21

REFLECTION FOR TODAY

Time spent dwelling on past situations or worrying about tomorrow's problems robs me of energy and lightheartedness and casts a shadow over all that today has to offer me. What I miss today can never be recaptured. Each circumstance and each experience of every day is meant to be a valuable aid in the fulfillment of my life. Living just for today and in today relieves me of stress and worry over situations which have not yet come to pass and of past situations which I cannot relive.

MEDITATION FOR TODAY

Help me remain within this day only so that I may enjoy to the fullest all that the day has to offer me.

TODAY I WILL REMEMBER

I only have today.

November 22

REFLECTION FOR TODAY

Sometimes when I live my life in the way necessary for me to maintain my wellness, I meet with other peoples' disapproval. At this time it is necessary for me to find out if I am harming any one. If not, I can quietly go about my business and continue to grow...without their approval. I know it is natural for me to want approval from my loved ones, but I must remember it is unhealthy for me to need and rely on approval like an addiction.

MEDITATION FOR TODAY

May I have the courage to continue to grow - independently of others' opinions.

TODAY I WILL REMEMBER

When I need others' approval before I can approve of myself, it is a reflection of my low self-esteem.

November 23

Using the Slogan "Look for the Good" has changed my whole attitude toward people, places, and things. Before EA my motto was look for the bad. I found flaws in everything. When I saw the negative, I never considered the positive. Now if some negative thought pops up, I try to replace it with a positive one. If something negative outside myself comes my way, I try to let it flow past instead of through me.

MEDITATION FOR TODAY

Let me feel pleasure in my friendships and activities by dwelling on the positives they add to my life.

TODAY I WILL REMEMBER

Look for the good; it is there!

November 24

REFLECTION FOR TODAY

Acceptance is hard to comprehend. I thought if I accepted something, that meant I liked it and I wanted it to stay. But this is not what acceptance is. Acceptance means being honest about what is happening in my life, what I am thinking, and what I am feeling. When I can stop denying and rebelling against myself, I can relax and let go of the control. When I stop trying to control, as the First Step suggests, I am open to the learning and healing which are waiting for me.

MEDITATION FOR TODAY

When I begin to reject myself, help me to stop for I am okay just as I am.

TODAY I WILL REMEMBER

Knowing that acceptance opens me to healing and learning, I will accept whatever I see in myself today.

November 25

REFLECTION FOR TODAY

I have come to realize that one of the ways in which I try to cope is to avoid all conflict and pain. What if today I found the courage to turn and face my difficulty? If I honestly and fearlessly looked at the person or the problem with a clear-eyed gaze, what might I see? I can believe that the person I fear could be a friend in need and that my problem, looked at in perspective, will melt away or diminish in size.

MEDITATION FOR TODAY

Please give me the courage to stop running away from life's problems. Help me today to deal with at least one of my problems openly and honestly.

TODAY I WILL REMEMBER

I will win by turning and facing my foe.

November 26

REFLECTION FOR TODAY

When I was emotional, that is living without the Program, I depended upon being right (at all costs) as my source of self-worth. I had to be right and in control of all situations, the center of attention. Now that I have the Program and the people in it to guide me along my way, I no longer need to be right; I need to be loving. I need to learn to listen and to share.

MEDITATION FOR TODAY

Oh, dear God, in all Your wisdom, love, and care, I thank You for taking me in and giving me rest from my perfectionism. I surrender unto You this self-centered attitude and fear of mine.

TODAY I WILL REMEMBER

Loving is the source of my self-worth.

November 27

REFLECTION FOR TODAY

My life was so confused and in such turmoil I never lived in my twenty-four hours. I was worrying or feeling guilty about something from my past so I never enjoyed life. I found I had a choice and changed my focus to today. My life is going on and the experiences behind me are the basis for my life. I am learning to take the negativity from these experiences and letting the positive take over. I know I must practice the Program one day at a time if I am ever going to get well. Even though I am sometimes confused, I can look forward to less turmoil each day.

MEDITATION FOR TODAY

Remind me that my past is something to learn from and not to dwell on.

TODAY I WILL REMEMBER

Improving my life is my goal rather than living and reaching out to false dreams.

November 28

REFLECTION FOR TODAY

How much time do we spend blaming others for the way we are? It may well be that our childhood experiences caused us a great deal of pain. But to continue blaming someone for the way we are only keeps us feeling miserable and hopeless today. This does not mean we should deny our hurt and anger. Neither should we blame ourselves. As we mature, we come to realize the people who hurt us were doing the best they knew with what they had been given. What can I do today that will bring me to a greater acceptance of myself?

MEDITATION FOR TODAY

May I remember I have the inner power given to me by You.

TODAY I WILL REMEMBER

Hope lies in taking responsibility for self today.

November 29

When I am open to growth, I discover many things about myself. At times it may seem as if this knowledge comes from outside but actually the knowledge has been within all along, waiting to be discovered. A growing person is attracted to those things which help him/her to go toward his/her greatest potential. As I have been willing to risk following the path which feels right, life holds challenges and adventures beyond my fondest dreams.

MEDITATION FOR TODAY

May I have the courage to follow my dream with action.

TODAY I WILL REMEMBER

I will be open to discovering another part of my truth.

November 30

The risk of caring is scary for each of us. It takes courage. We would like the love we feel for another to be reciprocated. When someone does not return our love, it can cause us to feel rejected. Rejection hurts. If we have felt cared about by someone over a period of time and that person withdraws, or worse yet, dies, we experience the deepest kind of hurt. This grief can make us want to close ourselves off from caring again. Yet if we refuse to continue being vulnerable, we will lose so much more. A part of us will die.

MEDITATION FOR TODAY

May I understand that the only way I will continue to discover myself is by caring for another.

TODAY I WILL REMEMBER

I will appreciate the value and care in my relationships today, for today is all we have anyway.

December

December 1

REFLECTION FOR TODAY

In the EA Program we are learning to live one day at a time. This can be confusing. Newcomers often say, "What about making plans? There are certain things which must be planned ahead." Of course there are life events that require planning. We say, "Make plans, but don't plan the results. Don't decide the outcome ahead of time. Put into action whatever is necessary to move the plan along and leave the results to your Higher Power."

MEDITATION FOR TODAY

May I become willing to be flexible and remember that You are in control of life now.

TODAY I WILL REMEMBER

I can make plans without rigidly trying to control the results.

December 2

REFLECTION FOR TODAY

How many blessings can I find to be thankful for today? It is easy to say, "Thank You, God" for the big things in my life such as: the recovery of a loved one's health, a new car, a job promotion, or the winning of a contest. But how about gratitude for the mundane or insignificant things such as: grass, getting home safely, being able to read the comics, or watch a favorite TV show? Certainly there are people in my life to be thankful for other than my spouse or significant other. How about the pleasant bus driver, a delightful co-worker, or the charming paper boy? There are things in my home to be thankful for - things which make my life easier and more pleasant. Air conditioners, dishwashers, and Scotch tape come to mind. Practicing gratitude throughout the day makes me aware of how blessed my life truly is.

MEDITATION FOR TODAY

Help me to remember to be grateful for all things large or small.

TODAY I WILL REMEMBER

Do not take my blessings for granted.

December 3

My life is occupied often with too much "thinking" and not enough "feeling". This condition of constant thinking leaves me physically tense at the end of the day. Usually this keeps me restless in my sleep at night. This physical discomfort alone should prod me into working the Fourth Step. Before I can free myself to feel, I must be willing to look at yesterday's hurts and guilts and put them on paper today. The unfulfilled needs of my infancy and the repressed pains of my childhood will slowly drain from me as I put to work the Slogan "Know thyself - Be Honest."

MEDITATION FOR TODAY

God, as I continue to understand You, please stand by me as I seek the courage necessary to work Step Four.

TODAY I WILL REMEMBER

Sustained healing takes place only when I work the Steps.

December 4

REFLECTION FOR TODAY

It is so much easier for me to forgive others than it is for me to forgive myself. I may have done something I believe is wrong, or failed to do something which should have been done, and for some reason, feel I cannot be forgiven. I need to remember my Higher Power will always forgive me and will give me the help I need to find the words and means to make amends to those I might have hurt, including myself.

MEDITATION FOR TODAY

If I am carrying thoughts and feelings of guilt and self-recrimination, remind me of Your forgiving love.

TODAY I WILL REMEMBER

Not to be so hard on myself.

December 5

REFLECTION FOR TODAY

In working my Fourth Step, I found one emotion constantly appearing - fear. Fear denied me the chance of enjoying my present surroundings and relationships. Fear led me to believe that upsetting experiences from my past would recur so I had to try and control the future. Fear limited my thoughts and actions like a chain attached to my body, dragging me down with its weight. Fear, in effect, stood boldly between me and my goal of serenity and peace of mind. I am learning to replace *fear* as the controlling force of my life with *faith* in a loving Higher Power.

MEDITATION FOR TODAY

May I let go of behavior and habits which I have clung to in order to handle fearful situations.

TODAY I WILL REMEMBER

Faith is action.

December 6

My defects of character cannot be removed by my will power. I have spent the better part of my life trying to combat these shortcomings. I have grown frustrated and anxious in the process. Steps Six and Seven say, "You have done your work in Steps Four and Five; now let go and let God. Just humbly ask for your shortcomings to be removed." As the Steps suggest, relax. I can now start to live a less anxious life. I can also start being more spontaneous and put my worries and emotional problems into the hands of the Higher Power.

MEDITATION FOR TODAY

May the faith I have obtained in the first Steps of the Program stay with me and help me to now complete Steps Six and Seven.

TODAY I WILL REMEMBER

Today I will relax my mind and body and truly accept that my Higher Power will remove my shortcomings at the right time.

December 7

REFLECTION FOR TODAY

If the weather is unpleasant, I will try not to let it ruin my day. When it is foggy and gloomy I will look for beauty in the difference of the scenery when objects are indistinct. When it is rainy or snowy, I will be glad I can stay inside or let it challenge me to dress appropriately and be comfortable in it. When the roads are bad, I will try to perfect my driving skills or see how I can plan less travelled routes.

MEDITATION FOR TODAY

May I look for positive things in whatever weather there is, accepting what I cannot change.

TODAY I WILL REMEMBER

Look for the good, even in the weather.

December 8

REFLECTION FOR TODAY

As we grow, we experience our worth and it feels terrific. We gain feelings of self-esteem and are grateful. Another period of growth comes along and we feel insecure and inadequate once again. We question and doubt if we have even gained any self-worth. It is imperative to recognize that personal growth, even after many years of growing, always produces feelings of instability. This instability can even border for moments on despair. Our willingness to embrace the struggle and to learn what we need to about ourselves will eventually produce an even greater realization of our worth.

MEDITATION FOR TODAY

May I be reminded that as I grow, self-worth will fluctuate and each new growth experience will grant me a deeper level of self-acceptance.

TODAY I WILL REMEMBER

I look forward to my next growth experience with hope.

December 9

REFLECTION FOR TODAY

So much of my grief is brought about by my own unrealistic expectations. Before the Program, I did not have guidelines or a Higher Power to help me find the balance between unrealistic and realistic expectations. High expectations of myself result in high expectations of others. When I fail to meet my own expectations, I feel I have failed. When others fail to measure up, I am angry or hurt. Low expectations of myself are just as damaging, and reflected in my expectations of others as well. Both myself and others are weakened if my expectations are too low.

MEDITATION FOR TODAY

Help me to see that a well-balanced outlook on what I expect of others and of myself will do much to eliminate my struggles with living comfortably and having meaningful, healthy relationships with others.

TODAY I WILL REMEMBER

I will strive for realistic expectations.

December 10

REFLECTION FOR TODAY

My tears have always been a source of shame.
When I was growing up I was told they were a
sign of weakness, self-pity, and foolishness. Con-
sequently I grew up fighting and repressing
them. In the past several years I have slowly
learned to accept them as an emotional release
and, most importantly, a source of healing.
When a grain of sand invades an oyster shell, it
causes irritation. Immediately the oyster
secretes a liquid much like a tear. This liquid
hardens and forms a globe protecting the oyster
from pain. The tear or liquid is called a pearl. So
my tears, too, are a beautiful and wonderful
function of healing.

MEDITATION FOR TODAY

Help me remember my tears are an expression of
my inner feelings and they are okay.

TODAY I WILL REMEMBER

My tears are pearls.

December 11

If I am powerless, my only reasonable course is to live and let live. I must learn, with God's help, to live my own life more fully and to let other people live their own. If I spend my time and effort learning to manage my own life, I will not have any time or energy left over to manage anyone else's. My reward is a feeling of freedom as my burden is lightened when I let go of what does not belong to me. I need not worry - God will take care of others.

MEDITATION FOR TODAY

May I remember that my progress comes from detaching from the idea that I alone can control other people or solve their problems.

TODAY I WILL REMEMBER

Mind my own business.

December 12

The Program is like a seed or young plant in the ground. If I am upset, I can't even think straight. It is important for me to quiet down, to be receptive to what is being said to me. First things first! To receive the message, I must be like the soft, rich earth - pliable, open, willing, and honest. Later on I have to weed out attitudes which can choke out sanity like anxiety and temper. For many, the promise of sanity is snatched away from them almost immediately by personalities taking over before principles have even had a chance to grow. Am I allowing the roots of my Program to go down deep? Am I "feeding" my Program with the spiritual nourishment provided by the Steps and Program literature?

MEDITATION FOR TODAY

Help me to absorb the sunshine of the fellowship.

TODAY I WILL REMEMBER

I will relax and watch my seeds grow.

December 13

The Second Step tells us we came to believe a power greater than ourselves could return us to sanity. In order to return to a place, one must have already been there before. In each of us there is a place, perhaps even beyond our earliest memories, where we knew the perfect harmony of mind, body, and spirit. Each of us is wonderfully made, designed to experience a vast range of emotions. Like high and low notes on a piano, like light and dark colors in a rainbow, it is the infinite range of possible variations which makes them beautiful and ever new. So, too, we need to experience *all* our emotions, high and low/light and dark. We then need to seek out in ourselves the place of harmony for each of them in our own unique range of self-expression. In EA that range is constantly widening, enabling us to "hear more music" and "see more colors" in our lives.

MEDITATION FOR TODAY

May I accept every emotion gratefully. May I acknowledge it, bless it, and allow You to help me interpret it.

TODAY I WILL REMEMBER

I am wonderfully made! As Shakespeare marveled, "What a piece of work is Man!" (Woman too!)

December 14

REFLECTION FOR TODAY

Not only am I powerless over some of the things which make my life unmanageable, but also over some things which make it manageable. For example, I am unable to alter, even in the slightest, my self-worth. My value as a human being is determined and fixed by God who has made me a worthwhile person and there is nothing I can do to change that. Nothing. However, my *feelings* about me and my worth do change from day to day, from moment to moment, because that is the way it is with feelings: they change. I am powerless over my emotions, including the emotion of self-esteem.

MEDITATION FOR TODAY

Help me to accept myself today as I am, even if my self-esteem is not as high as I would like it to be.

TODAY I WILL REMEMBER

My value comes from God, not from anything I do or fail to do.

December 15

REFLECTION FOR TODAY

Today I will accept my past. I will try to learn what I can from those experiences which cause me the most pain. I will be kind to myself, giving me credit for the things I have accomplished and not dwell on the things I have not done. With what I learn from my experiences and the will and strength of my Higher Power, I will try to make a better today and look forward to tomorrow.

MEDITATION FOR TODAY

Help me to accept and learn from my past so I can continue with my emotional and spiritual growth.

TODAY I WILL REMEMBER

Painful experiences are not shameful, but rather a way I can better come to know myself.

December 16

REFLECTION FOR TODAY

The verb resent comes from the Latin, meaning to feel again. When I resent someone, I recycle old anger, hurt, shame, and humiliation. This is just like sticking a knife into myself and twisting it. I toss and turn all night while the person I resent is home sleeping like a baby. The EA Program shows me the way out of this futile and agonizing self-torture. Powerlessness was my dilemma; today I have the power, through God, to forgive those whom I have allowed to hurt me. I can release myself from these burning resentments.

MEDITATION FOR TODAY

May I realize the more I resent someone, the more I hurt myself.

TODAY I WILL REMEMBER

To pray for those I resent, even if it is hard to do at first.

December 17

How I expend my time and energy during the day determines how I am going to feel about myself at bedtime. If I have used my time and energy in constructive and creative ways, I feel good about myself. If I have wasted the day in procrastination and negativism, I do not care very much for myself. When I am indecisive, I tend to procrastinate. If I have spent the day worrying about the past or the future, I have wasted energy, which leaves me physically but not mentally tired. I can choose early in the morning how I am going to feel late in the evening.

MEDITATION FOR TODAY

God, help me to do first things first.

TODAY I WILL REMEMBER

When one thing gets done, it is easier to do the second and the third and more.

December 18

REFLECTION FOR TODAY

I have heard that the eagle is the only bird who will fly into a storm. I like relating to the eagle because I know the quicker I face my pain, the faster I pass through the stormy time. On the other side of the storm I always find a beautiful rainbow. In this rainbow the colors show me the strength and courage which I had not known I possessed. This strength and courage gives me hope to face whatever lies ahead.

MEDITATION FOR TODAY

Grant me the spirit of the eagle so I can continue to soar and become the person You created me to be.

TODAY I WILL REMEMBER

Each time I face my pain I receive the gift of strength and courage.

December 19

REFLECTION FOR TODAY

I thought it was my responsibility in life to look for the bad. I thought I was supposed to look for everything wrong in every situation or person with whom I came in contact so I could tell them how to fix their problems. I put myself in charge. That is a tall order and a heavy burden. If I found everyone's imperfections, then they could change and would become perfect as I thought they should. If everyone did what I believed they should, I would not have any problems. This, of course, kept me from looking at me.

MEDITATION FOR TODAY

Help me to allow others to take their own inventories and to ask myself, "Whose problem is it?"

TODAY I WILL REMEMBER

I can find more joy in looking for the good.

December 20

We are used to the idea that death follows life. A less obvious progression which is very obvious in nature is that life follows death. Seeds must die in order to become plants. Caterpillars must die before butterflies exist. Old habits must die before new ones can be formed. In all of these cases the timing must be right. Then the old gives way to the new. As the old submits to this "death", our Higher Power supplies new life. As we work the Program we prepare the soil for the new life and we learn to know when the time is right.

MEDITATION FOR TODAY

As I submit to the death of the known patterns, I pray You will lead me to a new way of life with new patterns.

TODAY I WILL REMEMBER

Surrender and let God do it.

December 21

REFLECTION FOR TODAY

Confusion seems to complicate my mind when I want to make decisions. My Higher Power is there to help me sort out what is most important right now and I also have a Program to help me. Am I using it? My life has been lived through other people for so long my own worth and identity are lost at times. I can take time to relax and find out who I am and accept myself today. I am a valuable person, and at times I do not recognize it.

MEDITATION FOR TODAY

When I lose touch with my priorities, I know You will help me to see I must take care of myself first.

TODAY I WILL REMEMBER

I will choose to do the things which make me happy.

December 22

I am not always kind to people I meet. Some days I have to consciously work at being agreeable. I am not necessarily unkind, I just do not make that special effort to react positively. Those are the days when I am not particularly satisfied with myself. I am ordinarily a friendly, outgoing person. When I back away from someone I meet, it is me backing away from me. Then I realize it is time to act "as if" everything is okay - with me and with other people.

MEDITATION FOR TODAY

Remind me when I am being unfriendly I may be missing an opportunity to meet the best friend I could ever have.

TODAY I WILL REMEMBER

Life is a series of meetings; give them a chance to be meaningful.

December 23

REFLECTION FOR TODAY

So often I have held back from risking yet not understood why. I let fear control my life. Unless I challenge in the present my fear of losing love, control, or esteem, I will lose even more. Today is the only day I have. I will risk telling a significant person how I feel. I will also risk asking for something I have secretly been needing. And instead of losing, each time I risk I will ultimately gain.

MEDITATION FOR TODAY

May I remember that to risk nothing is to gain nothing.

TODAY I WILL REMEMBER

If I am open, I will gain more than I will ever lose.

December 24

REFLECTION FOR TODAY

Do I remember how it used to be a struggle to get out of bed in the morning because I just plain did not care? Do I remember how it was almost impossible to leave my home because of fear? How about the temper tantrums, crying spells, or days of pouting? It is not wise to dwell on the past but it is important to check my progress. I need to realize how much I have grown and how far I have traveled from my bottom level. Seeing the improvements gives me the necessary encouragement to carry on and certainly adds to my confidence and self-worth.

MEDITATION FOR TODAY

Help me to see how much better I am than I was.

TODAY I WILL REMEMBER

I will occasionally reflect on the "way it was".

December 25

REFLECTION FOR TODAY

For many people throughout the world, today is a day of celebration, giving and receiving, family gatherings, sharing and love, warmth and joy.

For many people, however, these occasions may bring out feelings of sadness, loneliness, depression, grief, and perhaps even a sense of hopelessness.

For any and all of us, perhaps it is most important in this holiday season that we accept ourselves and our feelings, whatever they are, and that we continue to believe and trust that we are not alone today.

MEDITATION FOR TODAY

Help me to try to retain and maintain love and hope today.

TODAY I WILL REMEMBER

Love is the most precious gift I can give and receive.

December 26

REFLECTION FOR TODAY

Our length of time in the Program can mean a lot or very little, depending on what we do with that time. The more we open ourselves to the healing of acceptance and surrender, the more growth we will achieve. On the other hand, we can sit in meetings for years and remain as closed and fearful as the day we came to our first meeting. At each meeting we have a choice. We can be open to the warmth and acceptance which awaits us or we can remain closed. Our Higher Power uses this time to touch us through each other.

MEDITATION FOR TODAY

May I be willing to do my part and not rest on my laurels.

TODAY I WILL REMEMBER

The gifts of growth and healing are available for me. I only need to accept them.

December 27

Many of us continue seeking relationships where we end up feeling rejected and abandoned. Yet we resist believing we could gravitate to relationships which could cause us once again to question our worth. It is a known fact, though, that we tend to repeat what we have experienced, whatever feels familiar. The familiar may be miserable but secure; we know what to expect. As we look honestly at our past relationships, how many times have we unconsciously been drawn toward someone who has not been able to be there emotionally over the long haul?

MEDITATION FOR TODAY

May my new awareness, plus Your guidance, help me seek relationships where I feel valued instead of rejected.

TODAY I WILL REMEMBER

I deserve to be valued.

December 28

To love someone is to give them something of ourselves. We risk being vulnerable; we want to share so much of ourselves. That person learns a great deal about how we feel and what we think. Our openness has given this person the power to hurt us. In sharing to this degree, we give up some of our personal power. Yet if we do not risk giving up some of our power, we will never experience what it feels like to be truly loved and cared about.

MEDITATION FOR TODAY

May I be willing to take the risk to love and to be loved.

TODAY I WILL REMEMBER

I would rather feel someone's love than have only my power.

December 29

REFLECTION FOR TODAY

There are times in our life when we want to give up. Our pain seems to have no end. In a sense we are like the runner of a twenty-six mile marathon on the twenty-fourth mile. The runner may think it is impossible to finish the race, or maybe lose perspective. Yet, if there is a reflection on previous efforts, the decision will be made, no doubt, to continue the race or at least give it one last try. It does not matter how many people come in before or after. It matters only that there was no giving up. When the runner crosses the finish line, the pain turns quickly into jubilation.

MEDITATION FOR TODAY

May I have the perseverance to continue my race.

TODAY I WILL REMEMBER

I will rejoice in my accomplishments. I will reward myself with something I enjoy, for I have done my best.

December 30

REFLECTION FOR TODAY

Often we rebel against our pain. In our painful moments we may feel very much alone; and it is true that to some degree we are. Yet, isn't it the pain which we have faced which has ultimately given us compassion for ourselves and then for others? Sometimes when we are open and share our pain, someone responds, "Thanks, you have really helped me." These moments create a deeper awareness of our value and the meaning to our pain.

MEDITATION FOR TODAY

May I have the courage to be open to what my pain is trying to teach me.

TODAY I WILL REMEMBER

Pain faced brings freedom.

December 31

REFLECTION FOR TODAY

"No matter what you do, I will still accept you" is a powerful message and a wonderful gift to hear from another. One might think this kind of acceptance would cause a person to act irresponsibly. Instead, this acceptance frees a person to experience what needs to be learned. Knowing someone is there who understands and cares ultimately helps one to become more honest and responsible.

MEDITATION FOR TODAY

May I be reminded that being loved and valued, no matter what one does, is necessary for a person's maturing process.

TODAY I WILL REMEMBER

I will be accepting of those I love. I will benefit, too, for I will become more loveable.

SUBJECT INDEX

SLOGANS WE USE

1. Let go and let God.
2. You are not alone.
3. Easy does it.
4. Live and let live.
5. First things first.
6. Look for the good.
7. But for the Grace of God.
8. Know thyself - be honest.
9. This too shall pass.
10. I need people.
11. Four A's
    a. Acceptance
    b. Awareness
    c. Action
    d. Attitude
12. I have a choice.

DON'T COMPARE

TODAY IS THE FIRST DAY OF THE REST OF MY LIFE

THE TWELVE SUGGESTED STEPS OF EMOTIONS ANONYMOUS

1. We admitted we were powerless over our emotions - that our lives had become unmanageable.

2. Came to believe that a Power greater than ourselves could restore us to sanity.

3. Made a decision to turn our will and our lives over to the care of God as *we understood Him.*

4. *Made a searching and fearless moral inventory of ourselves.*

5. *Admitted to God, to ourselves and to another human being the exact nature of our wrongs.*

6. *Were entirely ready to have God remove all these defects of character.*

7. Humbly asked Him to remove our shortcomings.

8. Made a list of all persons we had harmed and became willing to make amends to them all.

9. Made direct amends to such people wherever possible, except when to do so would injure them or others.

10. Continued to take personal inventory and when we were wrong promptly admitted it.

11. Sought through prayer and meditation to improve our conscious contact with God as *we understood Him*, praying only for knowledge of His will for us and the power to carry that out.

12. Having had a spiritual awakening as the result of these steps, we tried to carry this message, and to practice these principles in all our affairs.